ALSO BY MEZ BLUME

The KATIE WATSON MYSTERIES IN TIME SERIES

Katie Watson and the Painter's Plot
Katie Watson and the Serpent Stone

...

BOOK 4 Coming in 2020

KATIE WATSON AND THE CAGED CANARY

MEZ BLUME

RIVER OTTER BOOKS

First published 2019 by River Otter Books

Copyright © 2019 by Mez Blume

Cover Illustrations by Patrick Knowles

All rights reserved.
No part of this book may be reproduced in any form or by any electronic or mechanical means, including information storage and retrieval systems, without written permission from the author, except for the use of brief quotations in a book review.

PB ISBN: 978-1-9999242-6-3
EBook ISBN: 978-1-9999242-7-0

For Gordon. London has given me many treasures, but you are by far the best.

1

UPON A MIDNIGHT CLEAR

*D*o you ever have that tingling feeling that something important is about to happen? I do. In fact, I had that feeling for two months straight, right from the moment Imogen and I travelled back from the past. But every day that passed proved me wrong. Nothing ever happened.

Not *exactly* nothing. Life happened. I went to school, I wrote to Imogen in London, and she wrote to me. And finally, after a forever of days-in-which-nothing-much-happened, the Christmas holidays arrived and my parents put me on a plane to London. I was to spend Christmas with Imogen at my aunt and uncle's ridiculously fashionable town house, and I could hardly wait.

Finally, after months of writing letters, Imogen and I would be able to chat face-to-face about our adventure to the year 1828 and the friends we'd left behind in Cherokee Country. Finally, I would have someone I could talk to about the questions I'd been carrying around inside my own head for months, questions that boiled down to one name: Ramona.

The discovery that Ramona, my Cherokee great-great-great-grandmother, had been a time-traveller too and had passed down her gift of travelling to me had changed everything. The first time I fell through a magic painting and landed in the past, I thought it was just my luck. It might have happened to anyone. But now there was no doubt about it. I was special, and I don't say that to brag.

Since learning about my 'gift', something had weighed on my mind almost every second. Though I heard no voice, it was like someone was calling me to *do* something. I had a pretty good idea what that *something* was, though *how* I was supposed to do it was the greatest mystery I'd faced yet.

I had promised Ramona's family, Jim Weaver and Ka-Ti, that I would do my best to find her. But I ached to do more than just find her. I vowed to myself that I would bring her back to the family that had been broken by lies and misfortunes. As it turned out, *my* family. It was up to me to fix what was broken. After all, Ramona's sketchbook had come to me for a reason. It seemed that I was the only one who could put the broken past back together again.

But how? I'd never had any control over when or where I encountered a magic time-portal painting, or when or where the magic took me. So far, the paintings had sort of found me, as if the magic bound me to Ramona. I could only hope it would find me once again. In the meantime, I would just have to wait and watch for a sign, a flicker, a whisper of magic, and hope that when it came, I would be ready.

• • •

My first few days in London were a dream. Aunt Ginny took us Christmas shopping in Mayfair, ice-skating at Somerset House and treated us to high tea at Fortnum and Mason. Exhausted as we were after each day's festivities, our heavy eyelids never kept Imogen and me from staying awake long after we'd gone to bed, whispering about our own private concerns.

"I was thinking," Imogen said one night. "There were three months between your first time-slip (as she called it) and your second, right?"

"Right..." I answered.

"And it's *nearly* been three months since the last time..."

"Yea, so?"

"So maybe it's time! Maybe you're due another trip right about now!"

I mused over the idea for a moment. "I'm not sure it works like that," I said doubtfully. "But I hope you're right."

"Katie?" Imogen turned over to face me, propping herself up on her pillow.

"What?" I answered, alarmed by her no-nonsense expression bearing down on me in the darkness.

"Don't you *dare* go back in time without me."

"Trust me," I said, "I won't if I can help it."

She flopped back down on her pillow and sighed. "Good, because let's face it; you'll never be able to find Ramona without me."

I gave her shoulder a playful shove. "Well then, we'll just have to make sure we stick together."

"And keep your sketchbook handy," she added, "just

in case."

On Christmas Eve, Imogen and I pulled on our woolly sweaters, skirts and tights for Midnight Mass at St. Paul's Cathedral, a Humphreys family Christmas tradition. Someone knocked on the door. I pulled my sweater down over my head and opened it. Aunt Ginny stood in the hallway, her hair and makeup as perfect and glossy as a magazine model.

"I thought you might like to open this before we leave," she said, holding out a small, thin package wrapped in brown paper and red string.

"Oh. Thank you, Auntie." I took it, a little embarrassed that Aunt Ginny hadn't offered Imogen a gift.

She laughed in her tinkling sort of way. "It's not from me, dear. Here, it came with a card. Read it for yourself." She turned to go, calling over her shoulder, "Hurry, girls. We leave in ten minutes, ready or not."

"Oh, it's from a secret admirer, I bet," Imogen teased.

I grimaced at her and ripped open the card. I knew the handwriting instantly.

Merry Christmas, Watson.

Charlie still addressed me as 'Watson' in all his letters.

Sorry we won't get to see each other over the holidays. But I'm sure you and Imogen will get up to all sorts of mischief in London. I thought this little gadget might just come in handy if you stumble across any mysteries while you're there. Use it well.

See you in the New Year!
Love,
Your #1 brother, Charlie

"I wish I had an older brother," Imogen said with a sigh as she watched me peel open the brown paper. Inside was a slender leather case. I opened it to find what looked like an expensive, shiny blue fountain pen.

"Guess Charlie thought it would come in handy for taking notes in my detective notebook," I said, taking out the pen and clicking the end with my thumb. Instead of a ballpoint, a thin but strong beam of light shone out the other end.

"A penlight!" Imogen exclaimed. "That's way cooler than just an old fountain pen. Not to mention a great detective gadget."

Uncle Phillip called from downstairs.

"We're coming!" Imogen grabbed her purse and ran out the door.

I returned my new penlight to its box and tucked it inside my satchel alongside my detective notebook and, as Imogen had requested, Ramona's sketches. "Thanks, Charlie," I whispered as I slung the bag's strap over my shoulder and hurried out the door after her.

As soon as I stepped out of the black cab, my eyes soared upwards to the towering dome of St. Paul's Cathedral. Its shape reminded me of a giant bird cage set against a clear night sky scattered with happy, shimmering little stars.

"Katie, snap out of it." Imogen jostled my arm and I blinked at her, the dazzle of the stars still blurring my vision.

"Hurry up. They've opened the doors, and it's freezing out here."

"I never knew you could see so many stars in the city," I said as we shuffled forward behind the long line of tourists and Londoners crowding the cathedral entrance for Christmas Midnight Mass.

Imogen leaned her head back to look up at the sky. Thankfully, she'd given up the wacky hair dye and gobs of makeup, and I thought her naturally dirty blonde hair never looked better than it did now, in a long, Ka-Ti-inspired braid.

She gave an unimpressed shrug. "If you ask me, this display has nothing on the night skies in Cherokee Country."

With a glance over my shoulder at my aunt and uncle, I leaned over and shushed her. "Not in front of your parents, remember?"

"Don't worry. Mum and Dad will stay glued to their phones until the minute the service begins, mark my words. 'Tis the season for catching up on work, didn't you know?" she said dryly.

At last our turn came to step through the revolving door and onto the chequered marble floors of the cathedral. Had it not been for the other tourists' flashing cameras on every side, I could almost have believed we'd stepped through a portal into another world.

St. Paul's was the grandest place I'd ever set foot in, like the palace of some ancient Roman emperor. My eyes grew wide trying to take in the soaring marble archways, the golden chandeliers hung from the domed ceiling high, high above, the towering sculptures of angels and heroes.

We made our way up the centre aisle to find our seats. My eyes were again drawn up and up until my head spun. I felt like a tiny bug beneath that whale-sized dome and its colossal paintings of the saints peering down as if from heaven.

As we took our seats, Imogen pointed upwards at a rail encircling the base of the dome. "That's called the whispering gallery."

"You mean you can go up there?" I felt woozy at the very thought.

"That's nothing! See up there, the hole right in the middle of the dome?" She pointed to a circular hole, through which I could just see what looked like a smaller dome beyond the main one. It looked a world away.

"That's called the Golden Gallery," Imogen whispered. "I went up there on a class trip once. Nearly got sick from vertigo." She gave a little shiver and lowered her eyes.

As the first crystal voice broke the silence with 'Once in Royal David's City', my eyes continued their journey around the cathedral. It was my first visit to St. Paul's, and I wanted to take in every splendid detail. The choir boys processed up the long centre aisle and filed into the choir stalls, their candles glowing off the jewelled mosaics and pearly marble sculptures. All in a rush, that old tingling feeling scurried up my spine like electricity.

It's just the atmosphere, I told myself, rubbing away the

goose bumps prickling my arms.

But whatever I told myself, the feeling did not go away. It got stronger and stronger the longer we sat there under that dome. A nervous pulse began to tap, tap, tap at my temples, and it was all I could do to sit still through the service. At last the organ pipes bellowed out the last notes of 'Hark the Herald Angels Sing', the bishop gave the benediction and the sleepy crowds awoke from the spell of the music and candlelight. But not me. As those around me gathered their coats and shuffled slowly through the rows of chairs, I still felt spellbound... breathless, like I was standing on the edge of a vast drop.

In a daze, I got to my feet.

"Might as well sit," Imogen said through a yawn as she slouched further down in her chair. "Mum and Dad will want to speak to the bishop. He's a friend of theirs. We won't get out of here for ages."

I forced myself back down into my seat beside her and gazed up into the dome, my foot tapping the rhythm of my pulse on the tiles.

"Katie, are you alright? You seem a bit... jittery." Imogen was giving me a suspicious glare.

"I just have one of those feelings. You know, like I told you about. It's nothing." I said dismissively.

A conniving smile came over her face. "I've got an idea." She leaned in closer so as not to be overheard. "Want to see the crypt?"

I glanced around at the crowds of people being ushered towards the exits. "Are we allowed to?"

"Best not to ask," she said and sprung from her seat.

"Anyway, we'll just nip down there, have a quick look around and be back before anyone notices. I'll tell Mum and Dad we're popping to the loo and we'll meet them on the steps outside."

But Uncle Phillip and Aunt Ginny apparently wanted to speak to about a dozen important people on their way to the bishop. By the time Imogen got the chance to break in, most of the crowds had already disappeared out into the night.

We shook hands with the bishop as Uncle Phillip introduced us, then walked away as ladylike as we could, breaking into a run the second we reached the shadows of an enormous archway.

Imogen made a beeline for an open doorway, and we slipped inside without notice, turning down a broad flight of marble stairs.

The crypt was dark but for candles on wall sconces and chandeliers. Their flames danced into life as we walked past. The vaulted ceilings felt terribly low after sitting beneath the lofty cathedral dome. But all the same, the crypt was a vast world below ground, a maze of rooms, hallways and giant marble monuments. I was imagining how easy and how terrifying it would be to get lost down there when I caught sight of a painting in an alcove at the end of a long, candlelit hallway. While I stared at it, a voice whispered my name ... or so I thought.

"Im, was that you?"

"Was what me?" She spoke from behind me where she was bent over reading the inscription on a tomb. The voice must have been my imagination.

I turned back to the painting. It was small, too small

really to hang over such a grand table. I could hardly make out the details from where I stood, yet the earthy colours felt familiar. With apprehensive steps, I drew closer until I was standing close enough to see the picture clearly.

The candlelight shimmered on the painting's glossy surface, bringing warmth to the simple scene of an old beggar woman and a pretty young girl sitting side-by-side on the steps of St. Paul's and offering bits of bread to the pigeons.

"What is it?" Imogen stood beside me, head tilted as she examined the painting.

Without answering, I dug into my bag for Ramona's sketchbook, then frantically flipped through the pages until I found what I was looking for. Taking the page out, I held it up to the painting on the wall. My heart did a victory leap.

Imogen gasped and laid a clammy hand on my arm. "It's the same." She turned to face me. "But Katie, you don't think *this* painting could be...?" Her voice trailed off as our heads turned in unison, as if drawn by an invisible thread, towards the painting. I didn't dare blink, or even breathe.

Then, like passing into a dream, impossible things began to happen. A painted pigeon soared from the head of a sculpture and alighted on the old woman's outstretched arm. As she caught it, most unmistakably, her face wrinkled into a smile. Her head turned, and, next thing I knew, her bright, smiling eyes had found mine.

Before I could move, a whoosh of cold air whipped up through the passageway, snuffing out every last candle. In the pitch darkness, the cathedral did a pirouette. I was thrown off balance by an invisible force, landing hard on the marble floor, unsure whether it was my head spinning or my surroundings.

But as suddenly as the commotion began, it stopped. All was still, silent, and black as a starless night.

2

ONCE IN ROYAL VICTORIA'S CITY

"Ow," Imogen groaned nearby in the darkness.

I peered around for her uselessly. Then, all on their own, the candles lit up, first dimly, then strengthening to full beam.

I twisted around and found Imogen sitting a few meters behind me, her feet splayed out like a ragdoll's, rubbing a bump on her forehead. We looked at each other, neither of us speaking a word. We didn't need to. We both knew perfectly well that we were thinking the same thing.

I got shakily to my feet and helped Imogen up. We both stood on the spot, looking around for some sign of what had happened.

There was none to be found. The painting hung on the wall, just the same. The candlelight flickered against the marble and mosaics, just as before. *Nothing* had changed. We were right where we'd started.

But how could it be?

Imogen's utterly confounded face must have been a perfect mirror of mine.

"We're still here." She said each word slowly, as if she hardly believed them. "But I thought… then what just happened?"

As I opened my mouth, not knowing how to answer, the church bells began to toll midnight.

Like waking up from a daydream, Imogen gasped and scrambled down the passageway, up the flight of stairs and through the doorway into the cathedral. The entire place was empty! We shot down the chequered aisle floor for the main doors, but found them shut and bolted with a giant, wooden beam. Every last tourist and clergyman had gone.

"Now what? Mum and Dad will be looking everywhere for us," Imogen groaned.

I looked around, still half-dizzy, half-sick with disappointment to find ourselves in the same place, and just a bit relieved at the same time.

"Hang on," I said. "Didn't we come in through revolving doors?"

Imogen frowned at the carved wooden door. "I thought so too. Never mind. Help me lift this beam." She got both of her hands beneath the heavy wooden beam that barred the door from the inside. I followed her example and together we heaved it up and let it clatter onto the floor. While I looked around expecting to see someone coming to see what was making all the noise, Imogen found a handle of a smaller door built into the larger one. She gave it a wrench and, to my immense relief, the small door opened. We flung ourselves out into the frosty London air just as the bell tolled its twelfth and final gong.

The first thing that struck me was that the stars had

disappeared behind a thick blanket of cloud. The night sky, so glassy clear before, was a whirlpool of snow flurries. A freezing wind whipped the powdery drifts wildly about chimney pots, lampposts and carriages...

Carriages?

The old tingling feeling crept up my spine like icy fingers as it dawned on me. The London before my eyes had undergone a transformation. The cityscape before me belonged on the front of an old-fashioned Christmas card: snow flurries dancing in the misty light of gaslit lanterns; raggedly-dressed children laughing and hoisting snowballs at one another across cobbled alleys. In place of the bustling traffic of black cabs and red double-decker buses, a fanfare of stately, horse-drawn carriages jangled up to the cathedral steps where men in top hats and capes held out their gloved hands to women who gathered up long, bustled skirts before gracefully climbing in.

I blinked the snow from my eyelashes and turned to Imogen, once again seeing the same dawning realisation reflected on her face.

Before either of us spoke, a man's voice shouted, "Oi! You two!"

A man dressed in a blue, buttoned-up coat and a domed helmet was running up the cathedral stairs right for us, waving a truncheon threateningly as he came.

"Police!" Imogen grabbed my wrist and, together, we took off as fast as our shaky legs would go down the opposite side of the broad stairs, made slippery from the fast-falling snow. At the bottom, I chanced a look over my shoulder to see the policeman hobbling down after us.

"Come on!" Imogen urged, grabbing my hand and

whipping me around the corner of the cathedral. In front of us was a shadowy cemetery. We did our best to stay together, dodging and skirting our way through the snow-powdered headstones.

"Stop there!" the policeman's voice bellowed behind us.

We threw ourselves behind a big stone grave monument with the carved figure of a knight in armour sleeping on its lid. I hoped to goodness he would protect us from the policeman's view.

"Can you see him? Is he still coming?" Imogen panted.

I peered around the knight's pointed shoes. Against the misty gaslights, I could see the policeman's tall hat ducking and bobbing up among the headstones.

"He's looking for us," I answered. "We should run for it, before it's too late."

Imogen took a deep breath and nodded once. Then, like a couple of jack-rabbits running for cover, we sprang from our hiding place and sprinted. As we neared the east end of the cathedral, we both shot one last glance back at our pursuer. The same instant we turned back, a tall, shadowy figure arose before us like an apparition, but it was no ghost. Before we could stop ourselves, we hurtled smack into its very solid form.

"Sorry, sorry!" I mumbled as I tried to disentangle myself from the folds of his heavy trench coat. But by the time we freed ourselves, the policeman had caught up, spluttering and choking, snowflakes frosting his bushy eyebrows and moustache.

The figure in black stepped out of the cathedral's shadows. Before I could see his face, he lay a hand on my shoulder and the other on Imogen's.

"Inspector!" wheezed the policeman, his hands braced on his knees. "I apprehended those two peculiarly arrayed young ragamuffins slipping away from the crime scene just now." He pressed his hand to his chest. "They seemed in a mighty hurry, if you ask me."

The man in black spoke. "Thank you, Constable Smart. I will question them both forthwith." His voice struck me as surprisingly friendly, even polite.

"Shall I clap 'em in irons, sir?" the policeman asked, hopefully.

"I don't think that will be necessary, Constable," was the man's gentle answer. "They are securely in my custody, as you see. You had better keep an eye on the cathedral's west end. We don't want a thief slipping through our fingers, now do we?" As he said it, I thought his fingers tightened ever so slightly around my shoulder.

The policeman stood erect as a soldier, tipped his tall hat and marched back through the graveyard, twirling his truncheon as he went.

But the wheezing constable seemed the least of our worries now. Wasn't it just our luck to go and land ourselves in the middle of a crime scene? And this man in black, friendly enough though he sounded, seemed to have authority even over the police. If he suspected we had some part in a crime, how were we to explain ourselves? We hadn't even a clue what time period we'd landed in!

"Now, if you two young ladies might favour me with a

few minutes of your time, I'd like to put to you a question or two."

We both turned slowly to see, for the first time, the man in black's dimly lit face. I was amazed to find that it matched his voice – not in the least frightening, though he'd commanded so much respect from the constable. Deep lines creased his forehead, like someone who spent a great deal of time thinking. He looked down a hooked nose, and the bags under his eyes hinted he hadn't slept for many nights. But put all together, it was a kind, fatherly face. If anything about his looks made me uneasy, it was his eyes. They glittered in the lamplight beneath the brim of his black hat, sharp and unblinking as they floated between Imogen and me. I thought right away of the watchful eyes of a sleepless, wise old owl.

He was waiting, I realised, for an answer.

"Oh, um, yes. We'll try to answer your questions," I stammered.

"But we didn't have *anything* to do with a crime," Imogen added a little too hastily.

The man removed his black hat, methodically brushed the snow off the top, and replaced it. "Well then, it stands to reason that this interview should not take too much of your time." His whole face creased into a smile, then he reached his black-gloved hand inside his coat and pulled out a scrolled-up paper. Unfurling it, he held it out so as to catch the light from the streetlamp. "This picture is an engraving of a very famous oil painting. Are you familiar with the original?"

I bent over the engraving of a medieval king and queen with their court at a banqueting table.

Imogen took one glance and straightened up. "I've never seen it before."

The man in black turned his owl eyes inquisitively towards me. I looked hard at the picture – something did feel familiar about the Queen's face, but it was very difficult to see much detail in the dark, and I was not eager to raise his suspicions.

I shook my head. "No, I don't think I've seen it either."

He watched me sharply for an uncomfortable moment, then rolled up the picture and returned it to the inside of his coat. "Then it stands to reason you know nothing about how this painting came to be stolen from the cathedral and replaced by another mysterious painting, unknown to the cathedral chapter?"

"You mean to say that the painting was stolen from St. Paul's Cathedral?" I asked.

"This very night," he answered. "The cleric says the painting was in its usual place in the crypt before the Midnight Mass commenced. By the time Mass finished and the crowds emptied out, the painting had vanished."

Imogen fidgeted beside me, no doubt eager for our interview to end. But I had an uneasy feeling about this missing painting business, and I had to ask just one more question.

"I'm sorry. We don't know anything about it. But... just out of curiosity... did you say whoever stole the painting replaced it with another one?

He nodded one slow nod.

"I was just wondering... out of curiosity... what was the other painting a picture of?"

His eyes remained unblinkingly fixed on my face as he

answered. "It's a painting of an old woman and a girl selling wares on the cathedral steps. No one seems to know where it came from or who the artist might be."

I tried not to show my interest, but he must have heard me swallow down the large lump that leapt into my throat.

"You're quite sure you know nothing of the matter, Miss...?"

"Watson," I answered. "Katie Watson. This is Imogen Humphreys, my cousin. And yes, sir. I'm quite sure."

His mouth twitched. He seemed to be contemplating whether or not to believe us. I held my breath, expecting him to ask more questions. But after a second or two, his hard expression melted into a polite smile. "Very obliged to you ladies for your time. I shan't detain you in the winter elements any longer. If you see anything... suspicious, you will find me at this address." He handed me a card. "A merry Christmas to you."

"Thank you," I answered and, not knowing what was polite, I added an awkward sort of curtsey. Imogen followed my example, then took my arm and we set off at a quick pace. Not that either of us had a clue where we were going, but anywhere was better than a graveyard under the watchful eyes of the man in black.

3

DOBBS AND BETSY

I held the card up to the lamplight to read the engraving:

Sherringdon Janklow, Detective, 14 Portsmouth Street

"I can't believe it. He's an actual detective, which means he must be telling the truth about the stolen painting. But what can it mean? Whoever stole the other painting and replaced it with the magic one obviously did it for a reason…"

"Katie…"

"It's as if they wanted us to come here, to this very place and time. But how could they have known we'd see it? They're in the past… well, the present now… and we–"

"KA-TIE!"

Imogen had my attention. I snapped out of my thoughts and looked at her. She was standing in snow up to the shins with her arms wrapped around her middle, shivering. Only then did I notice that my own tights were soaked through and I couldn't feel my feet which had disappeared beneath the fresh fallen snow.

"Can we think about all that later?" she asked through chattering teeth. "We've got more pressing problems at the moment. Not freezing to death, for instance."

"Sorry, I guess I just... got a little distracted," I apologised, yanking one leg out of the shin-high snow. "You're right. We should get inside somewhere warm." I hobbled over the icy cobbles and linked my arm through hers, and together we pressed on against the gusts of stinging wind. I didn't look back, but I sensed St. Paul's dome still peeked over the roofs and chimney pots behind us, like a guardian watching over our retreat.

"I hate to ask, but where precisely are we supposed to go?" Imogen's teeth chattered as she spoke. "I mean, what's going to be open in the middle of the night on Christmas Eve?"

I raised my head, shielding my eyes against the fast-falling flurries. The street looked completely abandoned, the shop windows all dark or covered over with shutters. Here and there, a candle lit an upper story window, but there were no signs of welcome as far as the eye could see.

"Argh, let's just keep moving." Imogen covered her nose. "It smells like a barn out here. Or worse, a sewer. What is that stench?"

A shadowy movement in the alley to our left made us start. I thought at first it was a cat, but then I saw it was much too large. Now my eyes had dropped to ground level, I noticed to my horror that the street wasn't as deserted as I'd thought. Pressed up against doorways and into side alleys were groups of shivering bodies – men, women and even little children. It was no wonder we'd missed them before. They were all so dirty, they melted right into the sooty darkness of their hideaways.

One very young woman, no more than a teenager, huddled on the cold stone steps of a shop with two smaller bodies pulled close to her sides. On first glance, the trio were no more than a pile of dirty, tattered clothes in the shadows. But as we approached, three sets of hungry, hollow eyes turned upwards and caught the streetlamp's yellow light.

Seeing us stop and take notice, the young lady spoke. "Have a pity, misses," her voice creaked out like a rusty hinge. "Spare a trifle for my babies. For the sake of the Christmas child in the manger, have a pity."

We froze in our tracks, our eyes darting from the pitiful little family to one another.

"There's nothing we can do," Imogen whispered. "We don't have any food to share or warm lodgings to offer."

I bit my lip. She was right of course, but we couldn't just walk away and leave them to freeze either. I took my satchel off my shoulder and began unbuttoning my new pea coat. Imogen looked horrified, but after a deep breath, she too removed her designer white goose down coat and handed it to the young mother who gratefully took the coats and began bunching them around the half-frozen children.

"Wha's this? A couple o' li'l do-gooders, 'anding out Christmas charity," a gruff voice spoke from behind, and the young woman's teary eyes widened with fear. Imogen and I turned slowly around to see the owner of the voice. He was hideous. Though short, he was stocky as a bull. An oversized head rested right on top of his hunched, ape-like shoulders as if the weight of it had caused whatever neck there might have been to cave in. He approached, lifting the brim of his tattered hat to reveal a face that would make anyone wince: two bulging, blood shot eyes, a wide, leering mouth with more gaps than teeth, and a slash-mark scar across one scruffy cheek.

"Leave 'em be, Tobias. They ain't done no 'arm to nobody," the young woman pleaded. "They just gave what they 'ad to 'elp my babies, is all."

The stench of sour liquor and unwashed clothes filled my nostrils as the man advanced up the stone steps and jabbed his leering face up close to ours. "Is that so? Well then, what 'ave they got for old Tobias, eh? I'll bet there's a pretty li'l Christmas present just for me in that bag of yours, missy." He reached out and grabbed Imogen's purse with two monstrously strong hands.

How I wished in that moment I'd brought my blowgun with me! All I had was my own satchel filled with the precious sketchbook and my detective notebook. I picked it up, reared back and slammed it against the man's gargoyle-like head. He stepped back and lost his balance on the stair. As he teetered, Imogen yanked her purse out of his grip. Together we shot away as fast as our feet would take us across the slippery cobbles, pursued by the horrible man's bellowed curses. We never looked back but scurried on as quickly as we could, our eyes searching desperately for a refuge.

"Look, a light! Up there!" Imogen pointed to a large hanging light over a doorway. We skidded to a halt beneath the lantern which had on it in cast iron letters *Ye*

Old Cheddar Cheese Tavern. The windows were steamed up, but it was clear from the sound of laughter and singing there was life within. Imogen grabbed my arm and pulled me beneath a stone archway where a couple of drunken men staggered out the tavern door. We slipped around them unnoticed and ducked inside.

"Thank heavens!" Imogen groaned, bracing herself against the wall and doubling over to catch her breath. "You know, if I wanted to run this much, I'd join the athletics team," she panted. "Just as well we got rid of our coats before that hooligan turned up, huh? Katie?"

I wanted to answer, but my tongue was tied and my back pressed hard against the wall. The moment we had walked through the door, all the talking, laughing and singing had gone mute. Every eye was turned towards us, and none looked too cheerful. Imogen, becoming aware of our uncomfortable situation, zipped her lips and straightened up.

If there's one thing I admire about Imogen, it's her ability to take an awkward situation in her stride. While I might have stayed glued to the wall all night, or worse, run back out into the street, Imogen cleared her throat, thrust her nose haughtily into the air and took my arm. "Well *some* people *clearly* never learned that it is *rude* to stare. Come on, Katie. We've as much right to a hot drink on Christmas Eve as anyone else in here." And with that, she marched us right through the maze of tables, barstools and upturned kegs while the tavern's surly-looking patrons sneered and murmured to one another. Soon enough, as we wound our way through the series of rooms, they turned back to their conversations, laughter, shouting and alley-cat singing as if we had never interrupted them.

The tavern was a series of cavern-like stone-walled rooms with low ceilings that sank lower and lower beneath ground, a bit like a crypt. When at last we reached the bottom–a larger room with a crowded bar–we inched our way through the boisterous drinkers to where an old man with greasy grey hair was wiping down the bar with a grubby towel between swigs from a jug. After several minutes in which it appeared we were invisible to the man, Imogen boldly cleared her throat. He looked at us as if we'd just come from the lunatic asylum.

"Wot you want?" he wheezed.

"Are you still serving food?" Imogen asked with an impressive show of confidence.

"Bread and cheese is all you'll get," the man barked, gesturing towards a basket of loaves and a big wheel of cheese. My stomach gave a pleading growl.

"We'll take it. And two hot chocolates, please." Imogen sat herself primly on a bar stool to wait, but the man only glowered.

"You want hot chocolate, go to Fortnum and Mason. I've got ale and gin. Take your pick."

Imogen cast him a disdainful look. "Just the bread and cheese, then. And a jug of water."

The man still didn't budge except to hold out a dirty hand. "Pay first."

As Imogen resentfully clicked open her bag and dug around for her coin purse, I chanced a glance over my shoulder where I sensed someone watching us. I was right. A gangly boy in mismatched, misfitting clothes slouched against a wooden post with an unnaturally ugly bulldog at his heels, a tankard in his hand and an annoyingly smug smirk on his face. I caught his eye and he tipped his oversized top hat with a wink. I turned swiftly back to the bar, but I still felt the boy's eyes on the back of my neck.

Meanwhile Imogen and the bartender were caught at odds. "What do you mean it's not real money? These are pounds sterling. Legal tender!" Imogen was shouting.

"Look, Miss, I don't know who you fink you're kiddin', but wotever that is, you can't pay with it. Move aside and let the customers with real money through."

"I'm offering you way more than that bread and cheese are worth," Imogen argued, shaking a pound coin in the bartender's face.

"I said, MOVE ASIDE!"

"Now now, gov, don't bust a gut. You leave these bricky young lasses to me." It was the smug boy who spoke. He'd sidled up beside me at the bar as silently as a shadow while the bulldog snorted up behind him.

"Be my guest, Dobbs." The bartender waved his hand in the air as if happy to be rid of us, then turned to the next customer.

Imogen jumped off her bar stool and squared off the boy. She was taller by a couple of fists. "What did you call us? Something about bricks?"

"I meant no disrespect, Miss. Was a compliment about your being pretty bold for a girl 'n' all."

"Oh." Imogen looked appeased. "Well say what you have to say then."

The boy leaned in. "Step into my office," he said, beckoning us to follow him to a quiet back corner. With an overdramatic bow, he gestured to a couple of stools at a spindly little table before seating himself across from us. The bulldog snorted and threw itself adoringly on top of his feet. It was just as well; several of his toes had wormed their way out the holes in his boots.

Now that I had a better look at the boy, I thought he must be the most comical figure I'd ever laid eyes on. He appeared to have outgrown most of his clothes several years earlier, all except the oversized top hat perched atop his flyaway ears, and a chequered tailed coat that practically swallowed his gangly frame. He removed his hat to reveal a head of hair that looked more like pitched hay heaped about his impish, freckled face. There was no mistaking the mischief in his eyes, nor the half-grin that hinted he had some clever trick up his sleeve. One look, and I was immediately torn between a natural liking for the boy and an intense distrust.

Very suddenly, he thrust his fingerless-gloved hand across the table. "Name's Arty Dobbs, but most just call me Dobbs. And this 'ere is Betsy." The bulldog lifted her forlornly ugly head in acknowledgement, then flopped it down again.

We introduced ourselves, shaking his hand in turn.

"Wha's the accent?" he asked after I'd told him my name.

"I'm American," I answered a bit defensively.

He nodded knowingly. "Far from 'ome, eh?"

"She's staying with me. Now what did you want to say to us?" Imogen snapped.

"Oh, nuffink. Just, I couldn't 'elp noticing that the pair of you seems, well, out of place, shall we say. So I says to meself, 'Dobbs,' I says, 'what could two innocents like them be doing in this part of town without a chaperone on a Christmas Eve night?' Then I reckons to meself, 'they looks as though they could do with an 'elping hand.' And as it just so 'appens, mine is the most 'elpful hand a body could wish for. An' as it's Christmas an' all, I reckoned as I'd offer it to you. So, what's your predicament? Lost? Runaways? Criminals?"

"I don't see how it's any of your business," Imogen answered in her haughtiest tone.

"We need a place to stay," I said. I felt as wary as she did about giving away too much information to this strange boy; but we were in no state to pass up an offer of help. It might just be the only one we got.

Arty Dobbs sat back with an appraising look. "'Aven't you got a gov'nor or gov'ness? You're dressed strange enough, but never 'ave I met a street urchin wot looks like the two o' you."

"We're not urchins," Imogen retorted. "My father is a very important financier."

"Why ain't he lookin' after you, then?" Dobbs didn't miss a beat.

Imogen faltered a moment before replying haughtily, "He's away on business. As is my mother. We need a place to stay for the night, and that's all you need to know."

He bit his dirty fingernails in thought, then snapped his fingers. "I know just the place. Could take you there too… for a *small* token of… gratitude."

"You heard the bartender," Imogen snapped. "We don't have any *real* money, if that's what you mean."

"Thought you said your pa was an important financier."

Imogen shot him her iciest glare.

"Never mind," I said, pushing myself up from my rickety chair. "Come on, Im. We'll just find someone else to help us."

"Hold your 'orses." The boy put his hand out to stop us. "What about *that*?"

His eyes fixed on Ramona's sketchbook pressed tightly under my arm. While waiting at the bar, I'd slipped it out of my satchel to make sure the ape man's head hadn't done any damage to it.

"Looks like genuine leather. Book like that could fetch an 'efty price at the pawn shop."

I stuffed the sketchbook down into my bag, feeling fiercely protective. "This is *not* for sale. Let's go, Imogen."

We elbowed our way through the tavern and out onto the street. No sooner had we braced ourselves to face the snow flurries than the boy and his dog flew out in front of us, he blocking our way with his outstretched arms. "A'right, a'right. No need to get saucy. I'll tell you wot. I 'elp you now in the spirit o' Christmas 'n' all, and we agree on a suitable token of thanks later."

Imogen looked hotly sceptical.

"And what exactly is this place you intend to take us to?" I demanded, trying to sound tougher than I felt in that moment, shivering from a blast of cold wind and desperate for a hot drink and warm bed.

The boy crossed his arms over his chest with a smug expression. "A charity lodging for girls. 'S not far from 'ere. Run by a couple of spinsters, the Misses Turvey. I'll escort you there meself now and make introductions, 'ow's that?"

I could tell Imogen didn't trust this boy Dobbs, but, like me, was battling a desperate desire to believe there really was a safe, warm room awaiting us out there in the unwelcoming night. On the other hand, there was definitely something fishy about his over-eagerness to help... I felt certain he wouldn't be going out of his way unless he expected to get something out of the bargain. What if he really intended to lead us right into a den of criminals? From the looks of him, he was more likely to keep sewer rats for company than charitable spinsters.

After a moment's hesitation, Dobbs shrugged. "Unless you've got a superior offer..." He doffed his hat, bowed low so the shoulders of his oversized coat slid right up around his ears, then straightened up and, returning the hat, turned as if to walk away into the night.

At the very same moment, a shadowy figure appeared beneath the stone archway to the pub's entrance. A hulking, ape-like figure, breathing quick, raspy breaths like a rabid animal.

"Katie," Imogen breathed in terror, "Is that...?"

Two bloodshot eyes glowed in the lamplight.

"Wait!" I lunged for the boy and clasped his shoulder. He stopped and turned his impish, grinning face to me.

"Dobbs, right? We've decided to take you up on your offer after all."

4

A BOOK BY ITS COVER

*L*ondon was silent except for the echoing sound of Dobbs whistling 'Good King Wenceslas' merrily to himself as he led us down Fleet Street. Eventually, the dingy, overhanging buildings gave way to well-kept, stately brick ones. Up ahead, an enormous castle-like building rose up against the night sky like something from a fairy tale, and, in the middle of the wide road, an iron dragon perched on top of a tall pedestal as if guarding the way from enemy intruders.

"What is this place?" I whispered to Imogen as we passed under the dragon's shadow.

She peered up from the dragon to the castle. "Oh, I recognise this."

"I thought you said you was from London, Miss?" Dobbs said over his shoulder. "To be sure you must know the Royal Courts. All the fancy folk came out for to see the new statue put up for the Queen some years ago." He nodded towards the dragon statue.

I moved to get a closer look at the pedestal and noticed

the carved figure of a crowned lady holding a sceptre. "Is that Queen Victoria?" I asked.

Dobbs stopped in his tracks. Now it was his turn to look sceptical. "'Course, it's Queen Victoria. Who else? The Queen o' Sheba?"

Ignoring his sarcasm, I crossed over the road and began searching the pedestal up and down until I found what I was looking for. The letters MDCCCLXXX. I'd studied Latin numbers just last term at school and quickly worked it out. It was the date, the year 1880.

"I don't suppose you remember exactly how many years ago this statue went up?" I asked Dobbs.

He wiped his nose with his dirty fingers. "Matter o' fact, I do. Was the same year as me mum died o' the pox. I was seven then, 'n' I'm a man o' twelve now. You can do the sums for yerself."

"Five years ago," I said, then added with a meaningful glare at Imogen. "In the year eighteen-eighty."

She caught the look and her eyes grew wide. "Oh. You mean… it's eighteen-eighty-five?"

I nodded, then quickly smiled at a confused Dobbs. "Thanks, Dobbs. That's all I wanted to know. And I'm really sorry about your mum."

Dobbs shrugged. "S'a'right. She's better off in 'eaven than in the slums, like before. An' anyway, I'm better off than most o' the London Arabs who ain't got no parents, 'cause I got Betsy, 'n' Betsy 'n' me, we're as thick as thieves 'n' all."

"Did you say Arabs?" Imogen questioned.

"'S right. Street Arabs. You can't live in London 'n' not know 'bout us Arabs?"

"Well apparently you can," Imogen retorted.

Dobbs cast an incredulous look over his shoulder. "But there must be 'undreds, maybe thousands of us. Mind you, we stay 'idden well enough when we wants to, but still, you can't miss us. We Arabs is everywhere. Why, we own this city!"

"By Arabs, do you possibly mean… street children?" Imogen asked in a somewhat softer tone.

"If you like." Dobbs answered, walking along in the same confident gait. "Personally, I prefer Arabs, bedouins or the monkey tribe of the metropolis. You can take your pick."

Imogen and I shared a look of amazement. "Do you mean," I asked, "that you and these other Arabs don't have a home at all? But where do you sleep at night?"

"Wot, me?" Dobbs puffed his chest out. "We sleep wherever we please. Haycarts, railway carriages, rooftops when the sky's clear…" He talked as if these arrangements were a great luxury. "It's the rambling life for us, ain't it Bess?"

The bulldog bucked her enormous head and snorted in agreement.

I didn't know what to say. Dobbs was the same age as me, a boy of twelve, and hadn't a soul in the world to care for him, not even a place to call home, just like poor Oliver Twist. I thought all of that was just in books, but here was living proof that such sad things actually happened to children in London once.

We walked along silently for a bit, then Imogen tried to change the subject. "Your dog looks like she's seen better days. What happened to her?"

"'S the other way 'round, Miss," Dobbs replied with conviction. "Old Bess 'as seen worse days, 'n' plenty of 'em. She was bred for the fightin' pit, see. When she lost a fight, her old master left her in the pit to die. I found her nigh ready to give up the ghost 'n' managed to nurse her back to 'ealth, 'n', well, she's my dog now 'n' the best, most loyal dog as a body could wish for." He stopped long enough to bend down and plant a kiss on the scar-faced bulldog's slobbery cheek.

"Will she let me stroke her?" I asked.

"'Course!" He laughed. "She's gentle as a dove to friendly sorts."

I bent down and stroked back the bumpy folds on Betsy's forehead. She was pitiful to look at, but as her doggy eyes, so full of gratitude and contentment, met mine, I felt a lump rise in my throat. All in an instant, my distrust of Dobbs melted away. I straightened up, prepared to follow our guide in full faith. His heroic rescue of Betsy proved him trustworthy in my book.

The rest of the journey passed in no time with Dobbs telling tales of how he escaped from the workhouse and "took to a company of sailors" who taught him cards and magic tricks, and about the time he hung off the back of an omnibus all the way to the town of St. Albans before the driver noticed him and made him walk the whole way back to London. Only he didn't. He caught on to the first carriage that passed and rode into town "like the gentleman I am," as he put it. I forgot all about my numb, wet feet listening to his tales of cunning and adventure, and was just considering whether the life of an Arab was perhaps not so pitiable after all, when we turned a corner and Imogen exclaimed, "It's Covent Garden! Oh my gosh, I love this place. Mum takes me to the Royal Ballet just up there," she said, pointing.

Dobbs crossed his arms over his chequered chest. "I said I'd 'elp you, no questions asked. But if you don't mind my askin', I still can't see as 'ow you're in need o' charitable lodgings when you're a regular of the Royal Ballet? 'Aven't you got a fine 'ome of your own to go to on Christmas?" Dobbs wasn't giving up until he got some answers.

Imogen sighed, then replied coolly, "Fine. I'll tell you. My parents went abroad for Christmas and left my cousin and me with our horrible old aunt who beats us. So we ran away to find lodgings until they return. That's all," she added with a toss of her hair as if her far-fetched story were perfectly every-day.

Dobbs accepted the story without the least hesitation. "Glad as 'eck I 'aven't got an aunt like that. Come on then. Place is just around the corner, up 'ere on Long Acre."

"I've never seen Covent Garden this quiet," Imogen observed as we passed the columns and frosted glass of the market pavilion. The wind rattled the panes of glass and howled down the long, empty arcades like a ghost engine pulling into an abandoned train station.

Dobbs whistled. "Won't be quiet come mornin'. Christmas Day 'n' all, this place'll be positively 'eaving with business."

I'd almost forgotten! Tomorrow was Christmas. Our adventure to survive the night had driven all the festivity out of my mind. Normally I'd be bubbling over with excitement and unable to sleep on Christmas Eve, but at this point, all I wanted was a bed to fall into.

"'Ere we are!" He threw out his arms like he'd just performed a conjurer's trick. "Your lodgings, me ladies."

It was a tall, absurdly narrow brick building sandwiched between two larger buildings like a dill pickle between two buns. A sign hung over the front door, in bad need of fresh paint but still legible. Imogen read out the words – *The Misses Turveys' Hostel for Girls of Good Character* – then turned to Dobbs and asked, "Are you sure this is the right place?"

"Wot? You *are* of good character, ain't ya? Don't go tellin' me after we've come all this way that you're a couple o' she-pirates." He looked hopeful.

"Don't worry," I assured him. "We'll make sure the Misses Turvey don't find out."

DOBBS PULLED a string on the chipped red door and a bell jingled inside. When a moment passed and nothing happened, Dobbs reached up to pull the bell again. Just as he did so, the door creaked slowly open and two very different faces peeped out at us, each topped with a frilly night cap.

A pinch-faced lady squinted doubtfully at us. "What is it? What do you mean by disturbing us at this hour, and on Christmas?"

"Oh Agatha," the other, a soft, smiling lady, said. "They're only poor children."

Dobbs doffed his top hat and made a sweeping bow. "A Merry Christmas, Miss Turvey. Miss Turvey. Arty

Dobbs at your service." He stepped aside and gestured to the pair of us. "I've brought a couple o' girls o' the very best character wot as find themselves in need of lodgings. Might you 'ave any place for 'em?"

The pinch-faced Miss Turvey stuck her candlestick through the crack in the door to light up our faces, then dropped the light to look at our clothes. Her eyes widened behind her half-moon spectacles. "From whence, may I ask, do these girls come?"

Dobbs stepped in and explained the sad story of our abusive aunt. "Won't be but a few days afore this one's parents return to London, an' 'er pa will be that grateful to you. 'E's an important... uh... wot was it, Miss? A fine-nan-seer?"

"He's a financier," Imogen corrected. "And I'm sure he'll be very happy to pay you for our time here when he returns."

Inwardly I cringed, knowing the payment would never come. But from the changed expression on the lady's face, Imogen's assurances had done the trick.

"Oh, well. In that case." She opened the door and said in a much more genteel tone, "Do come inside, my dears."

On the threshold, I stopped and turned back to Dobbs. "But where will you go?" I asked. "You can't sleep outside in this weather. Couldn't we ask if you can stay here too?"

Dobbs looked scandalised. "I can't stay 'ere. It's for *girls!*" He gestured to the sign as if I were thick. "Don't worry 'bout me, Miss. There's a shed for livestock just the other side of the market–"

"Livestock?"

"Ya know wot livestock is, don't ya? 'Orses, goats, pigs, sheep…"

"I know what livestock is," I interrupted. "But what's that got to do with anything?"

"Ah, well, I was gettin' to that, wasn't I? Samson – 'e's a cart mule wot's kept in that shed – not treated too well, mind, so 'e's always 'appy to see Bess 'n' me." He scratched his head. "Not that 'e *can* see very well. Only got one eye, see?"

I shook my head. "Wait. So you're spending the night with a one-eyed cart mule?"

"'Course!" he said. "Bess 'n' me'll sleep like roy'lty in all that hay." Before I could say another word, he tipped his hat and leapt down the steps two at a time with Betsy lumbering after him.

I watched the pair of them disappear into the shadows to the whistled tune of 'Good King Wenceslas' and felt a swell of gratitude mixed with amusement. Dobbs had been true to his word. He had helped us without another mention of the 'token' for his trouble.

In the future, Katie, I scolded myself, *don't be so quick to judge a book by its cover.*

5

THE MISSES TURVEYS' HOSTEL FOR GIRLS OF GOOD CHARACTER

"Come in. Come in. Let us get you out of that snow!" It was the other Turvey sister who now bundled me through the door, throwing her own shawl over my shoulders. We stood just inside the door in a dark, poky hallway at the foot of a dark, narrow staircase.

The Turvey sisters' up-lit faces seemed to hover in the darkness, eyeing us. I thought again that the two could not have been more different. The one was long and thin, like stretched taffy. Her large watery eyes blinked at us behind her spectacles as she dabbed her long nostrils with a handkerchief. Her grey hair was pulled so tightly beneath her nightcap that it gave her an even more stretched, dismayed expression.

The other Turvey sister looked as soft and plump as a peach. Her head hardly reached her sister's bony shoulder, but her full, round face, framed in little white curls, smiled adoringly up at us. It was she who spoke first.

"I'm Effie Turvey and this is my sister Agatha, and you are very welcome to our home." She smiled all the time she spoke. "The house was left to us by our late father, the Reverend Aldous Turvey," – as if on cue, she raised her candle to light up a portrait on the wall of a sombre-looking man with bushy lambchop sideburns – "who devoted his life to bringing the Good News to the people of China." Lowering the candle to her rosy face, she continued, "We have dedicated this house to helping poor and needy girls in honour of his memory." She finished the speech with a little curtsey. "And what might your names be?"

"I'm Katie," I answered, and this is my cousin –" Imogen's stomach gave a magnificent growl.

"Imogen," she finished sheepishly.

With a gasp, Effie took Imogen's and my hand in each of hers. "Poor lambs! Bless my soul but they look half frozen, do they not, sister?"

"I'm sure they do, sister," Agatha croaked, grasping the banister post with one hand and laying the other, which clung to a frilly handkerchief, against her forehead. "I could hardly be expected to notice, my nerves are so very rattled. Of course, I wouldn't dream of complaining about being woken from a sound sleep in the middle of the night, and at my fragile age. 'Tis our charitable duty to suffer like the martyrs of old, and," her watery eyes turned dramatically towards the ceiling, "I count myself a martyr."

Effie Turvey released our hands to take her sister's and pat it, nodding sympathetically. "That's just what you are, sister. A martyr."

"'Tis true." Agatha nodded piously. "But you'll not hear a word of complaint from my lips."

"No one would dream of it, sister," Effie assured her.

"I won't say a complaining word about it, but my nerves are so severely shaken, I've no choice but to return to my rooms." She turned her enormous blinking eyes towards us. "Effie will show you to your own room and see you settled. She is fortunate not to suffer as I do from such afflictions as nerves."

Effie shook her head sorrowfully. "'Tis very hard for you, sister. But never you mind. I'll see these two sweet angels settled."

Agatha stepped lightly onto the first stair, then stopped and turned. "Breakfast is at 8 o'clock sharp if you want it. I spend that hour in private contemplation and prayer, but Effie will see to your needs." And with that, she climbed the stair with her candle and her head held aloft as if she were ascending the heavenly stairway.

Effie led us along the poky corridor to the back of the house, then down an even pokier flight of stairs and into a draughty cellar kitchen with stone floors and a small, smoking fire.

Imogen and I were seated side by side on a wooden bench at a long table. We watched while Effie, after tying an apron over her nightgown, bustled between a small cupboard and the feeble little fire and, like a fairy godmother, conjured up a loaf of bread, a hunk of cheese and two steaming bowls of leek and potato soup.

"Now, don't you waste any ladylike airs on me. You're hungry, so you slurp up that soup as quick as you can." She leant down and added in a whisper, "Besides, Agatha's not here to know."

We thanked her, then did just as she ordered us,

plunging our spoons into the hot soup and slurping it up. Only when I'd finished the bowl did I sit up to enjoy the wonderful sensation of thawing insides. Effie watched us with delight.

"It was delicious," I said after slurping up the last bit of broth, which made her beam all the more.

"Well, I suspect now you're fed, a warm bed is what you need most. Your room is right at the top of the house, but when the fire is stoked, 'tis as snug a little room as you could wish for."

She led us up the creaky flight of stairs to a landing where she put her finger to her lips and mouthed "Agatha." We tiptoed past the door behind which Agatha was already snoring like a bear, then followed up another flight of even creakier stairs to the attic. Effie pushed open the door into a tiny room with slanted ceilings, a bed and a miniature desk. It was cold, but in no time she had a fire going in the grate and the room became friendly and snug in its glow, just as she'd said.

"Now," she brushed her hands off as she rose from the hearth and smiled. "You've a candle allowance of two per day. Tapers and matches are kept in the desk. And you'll find two nightgowns laid out on the bed. As for day clothes ... I suppose what you're wearing is all you have?" Her eyes flitted over the damp short skirts, tights and sweaters we'd travelled in. "Your garments are of a most ... *interesting* fashion. But perhaps you'd be more comfortable in something else? I'll just have a look in our charity cupboard. We've just had a delivery from the girls' school, so I'm sure we'll find something to suit you both. Leave it to me."

We thanked Effie again as she left, glowing all the way out the door. Once we were alone, we wasted no time in pulling off our wet things and getting into the woollen nightgowns left out for us, along with floppy little nightcaps. We pulled them on, then looked at each other and laughed.

"Welcome to jolly old England!" Imogen said, pantomiming a curtsey. "Let's see what 1885 looks like from here." She creaked across the floor to the window and knelt on a stool. "It's awfully grubby," she said, using the outside of her fist to wipe clear a portion of the soot-coated glass. "But what's a little grime?"

I flopped onto the bed. "I never thought I'd hear *you* say that."

She looked mischievously over her shoulder. "After sleeping beside a muddy river night after night last October, this is nothing."

"I've been thinking about that, actually. I mean about what happened in Nickajack ... I just can't work out how it all fits with *this* time. We got here by following one of Ramona's clues from her sketches," I began, hoping to untangle my thoughts by speaking them out loud. "Our mission is to find Ramona. She's the key to getting home, but also to this whole great puzzle of why I time travel." – with every word, I felt more certain, and my pulse rushed a little faster –"She *must* be here, Im. I just know it." I caught her eye and paused. "Are you smiling?"

"I can't help it," she said, grinning. "I know it sounds mad, but ever since we got back from 1828, I've kind of been wishing it would happen again. That trip was the best time of my life."

I could hardly believe my ears. "You *do* remember how we nearly died on several occasions? And snakes. There were lots of snakes."

"That just goes to show how this time is going to be even better. No snakes in England!"

I couldn't help laughing, in spite of my nervous pulse. "I'm glad you're here, Im. I never thought *you* would remind *me* to relax and enjoy the adventure."

She shrugged. "Well, I learned that lesson from a very wise cousin of mine. But enough sentiment. My feet are cold." She tiptoed back across the creaky floorboards and climbed under the blanket. "Now, where do we start to solve this stolen painting mystery, Watson?"

"Right, the painting." I rubbed my palms together, eager to dive into a fresh, new mystery. "Who would steal a painting on Christmas Eve night?"

After a pause of pin-drop silence, Imogen said, "We don't exactly have much to go on…"

"You're right," I admitted. "And not much to go on to find Ramona either. This city is huge. But…" – I pulled my satchel into my lap – "hopefully the sketchbook will lead us in the right direction." Throwing open the bag's flap, I reached in and froze.

"What's wrong?" Imogen leaned forward to peer inside the bag.

My mind drew a blank so that all I could say was, "It's not here."

"What's not?"

"The sketchbook. I had it in my bag and now it's gone. There's only this." I pulled out a piece of splintered wood that was roughly the size of the sketchbook and held it up in horrified disbelief.

Imogen frowned at the imposter piece of wood. "When's the last time you saw the book?"

I closed my eyes, trying to remember. "When that boy, Arty Dobbs asked if... Wait a second." My stomach sank. "Surely he didn't..."

"What?" Imogen urged. "You don't think he...?"

Slowly, with a sickly feeling creeping into my stomach, I nodded. "You saw the way he was eyeing it. He *must* have stolen it." The chunk of wood dropped to my lap. "And to think I trusted him all because of his dog rescue story."

"That little weasel!" Imogen snarled, punching her palm with her fist. "Just wait 'til we meet again." She made a violent face as she strangled an imaginary neck in front of her.

"Without that sketchbook, we have *nothing* to go on," I said, letting my head collapse into my hands.

"Oh, we'll get it back. You'll see," Imogen said through her gritted teeth. "Arty Dobbs is about to find out just how *bricky* I am."

6

CHRISTMAS GOOSE CHASE

I fell asleep that night fuming. If Arty Dobbs wasn't pricked by his conscience, I hoped at the very least he was out there somewhere sleeping in cold manure and being pricked by bits of frozen hay. It was too much to stomach how he had pulled the wool over my eyes and stolen from me in cold blood. But if I was angry at Dobbs, I was even angrier with myself. I, who was supposed to be a seasoned detective by now, had fallen for his tricks like a mouse for the old cheese-on-a-trap trick.

I don't know when I fell asleep, but I woke with a start to the bizarre and unexpected crow of a rooster and the frosted window glistening from pale morning rays. It took a few blinking moments to remember where I was – *a rooster in London?* – before the memories of my stolen sketchbook came back to me, and all my anger came flowing back with it until I was wide awake and ready to pounce.

I shook Imogen's shoulder.

She might as well have been a brick.

"Merry Christmas!"

Miraculously, one of her eyes peeled open and searched around the room.

I gave her a minute to re-orient herself before asking, "Ready to catch a thief?"

At that, her eyes opened wide and, in a most un-Imogen-like fashion, she threw off the blanket and sprang out of bed. Then, with a gasp, she jumped back into the bed and flung the cover over her legs. "It's freezing!" she stammered, teeth chattering.

There was a tap on the door. Effie Turvey's round, rosy face appeared, topped with a lacy, lilac mopcap. "Oh, good. I was afraid of waking you."

She backed into the room carrying a big, wicker hamper. "Merry Christmas, dears. I've picked out a few items from the charitable donations for you. I hope they'll do."

She set down the hamper and began to poke the fire. "The basin's on the desk if you want a wash. Most of the other girls have already taken to the streets to look for the day's work, but there are still plenty of currant buns – a little Christmas treat – and a pot of hot coffee in the kitchen. Now, I'll leave you to it. I must tend to poor Agatha. It seems her rheumatism is keeping her in bed this morning, poor lamb. And on Christmas!" Her smile dropped for just a moment in which she looked on the verge of tears; but the next second her chirpiness returned. "Do help yourselves, my dears."

We wished her a merry Christmas and thanked her for the clothes as she backed out of the room nodding her frilly head.

"Did she say the other girls had gone out to find work?" Imogen looked scandalised. On Christmas?" She shook her head as she tiptoed across the chilled floorboards to kneel on the hearth mat and began picking through the clothes hamper.

"I guess Christmas isn't a day off for poor people in 1885," I answered, leaning on the window ledge and peering down at the bustling scene below. "And you know what that means?"

Imogen dropped the plaid dress she had been considering and twisted around. *"What* does it mean?"

I turned to face her. "It means, Arty Dobbs has more than likely already hit the streets as well. There's no time to lose if we're ever going to find him."

Imogen snorted. "I wouldn't worry *too* much. He's pretty recognisable with that ridiculous top hat, those dumbo ears and that mangy dog always at his side. Not to mention he must reek of livestock after having a sleepover with them."

"I'm not so sure." I gestured her towards the window.

Her perplexed face fell as soon as she gazed out. "Oh crumbs!" The deserted streets from last night had transformed into something of a carnival. Covent Garden Market vibrated with life: carriages, carts, people and animals.

Imogen pushed herself away from the window and cracked her knuckles. "Well, what are we waiting for? Let's get Victorian."

Somewhere, church bells clanged the nine o'clock hour as

we left the Misses Turveys' Hostel for Girls of Good Character to join the London mobs, and did we ever look the part. Imogen wore a violet dress with pearly buttons up the front, and I'd chosen a simple blue chequered one with a fat blue ribbon around the waste. Once we wrapped our torsos with crocheted shawls and stuffed hot currant buns into our dress pockets to warm our hands as we set out into the frosty streets, we were armed and ready to hunt our criminal.

Shutters still covered the shop windows, but that didn't stop street sellers from making the most of the festive mood to sell their goods.

"Holly and Ivy for your doorways! Mistletoe for the Missus!" a woman shouted as she swayed from door to door with a basket of greenery perched on her hip.

Across the road, a man pushed a cart full of dead birds along the bumpy cobbles. "Get your Christmas goose! Fattest birds you'll find in London!"

A pair of cantering horses brought a carriage careening in his direction. He swerved, sending a puff of white feathers into the air, swirling about like giant snowflakes.

"Drive on!" a smartly dressed man inside the carriage called out. The driver gave a choked *"YA!"* as he batted away the attacking feathers.

"How are we supposed to find one boy in all this madness?"

I was busy searching hopelessly for an answer when a shrill whistle blew. A policeman with a blue uniform and tall hat was darting through the crowds and carts in the middle of the street, heading in our direction.

"Stop that crook!" he shouted, pointing at someone a

little way ahead of him. It didn't take long to discover who it was. A tatty top hat was weaving its way through the crowded street, darting madly this way, then that, like a kite caught in a gale. The hat turned behind what appeared to be a sort of horse-drawn bus and disappeared.

Recalling Dobbs's boastful tales of omnibus getaways, I deduced that the horse-drawn vehicle must be an omnibus, which meant it was very likely…

"Come on," I said, grabbing Imogen's hand and plunging headfirst into the current of shoppers and sellers.

Keeping up with the omnibus was not difficult. It stopped several times to let people on and off. We kept a close distance, watching for any sign of a top hat or a bulldog getting off each time it stopped.

The bus started off again, and we started after it when Imogen threw out her hand. "Wait, it's turning." We watched as the bus turned down a side street. Sure enough, there, hanging off a hand rail, was the unmistakable Arty Dobbs, and there on the back step sat his loyal partner in crime, Betsy. Dobbs held an apple in his free hand, chomping off mouthfuls as if he hadn't a care in the world.

"Hey!" a policeman across the street shouted out. We weren't the only ones to spot the fugitive when the bus turned its broadside to our view. Dobbs tossed the apple, raised a hand to his hat, and pushed himself down out of sight.

"Ugh, great! He's giving them the slip," I groaned. "If we hurry, we can get in front of the bus and ambush him when he gets off."

Paying no attention to the scandalised expressions of

well-to-do passers-by, we hoisted up our long skirts to slosh across the slushy road as quickly as we could. Then we darted down the side road after the omnibus, passed it and slipped in a narrow side alley between two tall buildings to wait out our prey.

Imogen peered around the corner.

"Can you see him?" I panted.

"Yup. He's... oh! He's getting off! He's coming this way. Get ready to grab him."

Dobbs's clear-toned whistle came first, growing louder by the second and accompanied by Betsy's snorts. So, he was taking an "act natural" approach to throw off the police.

Imogen held up a finger and mouthed silently, "One-two-THREE!"

On three, we both sprang from our hiding place, grabbed whatever bit of Dobbs's clothing we could get our hands on, and yanked him into the alley.

Imogen, who was taller and stronger than the gangly street boy, pinned him up against the brick wall by his coat collar. The violent action brought out a side of Betsy we had not seen before. She growled low and bucked her hind legs as if about to charge Imogen. I froze, worried that Dobbs might give the signal to attack.

"He went this way!" a voice shouted from the road. Footsteps were running in our direction.

"Shush, girl," Dobbs whispered hoarsely. "Play dead." To my relief, Betsy whimpered and flopped over on her side. The policemen, meanwhile, were getting close.

Dobbs cast me a pleading look. "You wouldn't give me away to them square-keepers, now would'ya? Not after I 'elped you out of a fix 'n' all?" Now he was at our mercy, his bravado was deflating like a balloon shot by a blowgun dart.

Imogen gave me a quick nod. I nodded back, then stepped out of the alleyway just in time to meet the pair of policemen. They pulled up short when they saw me.

"Are you looking for a boy in a hat with a dog?" I asked.

"Tha's right," one of them answered. His red face sparkled with perspiration. "Stole from the grocer. You see which way he went?"

I nodded. "He crossed the street, I think, then headed back to the main road."

The red-faced policeman grimaced at his partner. "I told you he'd have a trick up his sleeve. That one's a right skilamalink. Manages to slip through our fingers every time. But just you wait." He shook his fist at an imaginary Dobbs. "Your fun is comin' to an end, ye young ruffian." He tipped his hat to me with a "Ta, miss," and the pair of them turned on their heels and chugged and huffed back the way they'd come.

No sooner had I ducked back into the alley than Dobbs gave a low whistle. "Well, fancy meetin' the two of you 'ere. Why 'tis jus' like a Christmas miracle, make no mistake. An' if I may say, you're both lookin' much better for the night's rest." His wide, mouth stretched into a sheepish, crooked grin. Imogen kept him pinned to the wall with her fists at his throat.

"I'll tell you what," he went on, his confidence not the least bit deflated. "Being the generous businessman that I am, I'll call us even now, on account of your 'elp. We can forget all about that little token we was to agree on. What do you say, an 'elping hand for an 'elping hand?" He struck out his dirty hand to Imogen as if expecting her to shake it.

She simpered and released her grasp on his collar. Taking his out-held hand in hers, she yanked it hard so the two of them were nose to nose. "You call that even? Not even close. You stole something from us."

Dobbs looked scared, then wounded. "Wot? Me? Steal from a couple o' gentle ladies such as yourselves? Me? The gallant gentleman who went out of me way to find shelter for ye just last night? Me, who never took wot wasn't mine in all me life –"

"Oh please. Give it a rest." Imogen kept Dobbs fixed with her steel blue eyes and iron grip on his hand. "Search him, Katie," she ordered.

I rummaged through the pockets of his coat, his trousers and the little cloth bag he wore slung over one shoulder. What I found was a walking curiosity shop. His pockets were stuffed with handkerchiefs, wallets, rings, plums, coins ... I pulled out a lacy hanky with flowers and initials embroidered in pink and held it up to his face. "*This* is yours?"

Dobbs shrugged sheepishly. "Wot? I like fine things as much as the next gent."

I stuffed the lacy hanky into his coat lapel. "All right. Where's the sketchbook?"

Dobbs pretended to be perplexed. "Skitch... sketch... wot was it?"

"The leather folder you stole from us," Imogen growled, tightening her grip on his hand so he winced.

"Hand it over now or we'll call those policeman back over here and see what *they* make of your collection of *fine things.*"

Dobbs took the threat to heart. His confidence drained along with the colour in his flushed cheeks. "Thing is I... I don't 'ave it anymore."

Imogen gave his hand another hard squeeze. "Liar."

"That's the honest truth! I admit I took it, but... I sold it."

Imogen looked ready to pound his lights out. "Sold it? You little—"

"Wait a second, Im." I stepped between them and gave Dobbs a hard, squinting stare. For all we knew, this might be another one of his cunning acts, and I wasn't about to fall for it again. "How could you have sold it? It's Christmas Day. The shops are all closed."

"Christmas don't stop *'im* doin' business, do it?" he answered enigmatically.

Imogen and I exchanged a confused look.

"Stop who?" I demanded.

"The one wot I sold your sketchbook-fingy to." He lowered his voice as if in deference. "The Old Bargeman."

"The *who?*"

"The Old Bargeman," he repeated more loudly. "Calls 'imself Capt'n Nemo. Buys and collects all manner of art 'n' antiques 'n' fings."

Imogen grabbed Dobbs by the collar again and looked him square in the eye. "Now you listen to me. You're going to take us to this bargeman, Captain whatever-he's-called, and explain that that sketchbook was not yours to sell."

Dobbs laughed nervously. "Can't do that, miss."

I crossed my arms over my chest. "Imogen, you've got a louder voice than I have. Call for the police, will you?"

"With pleasure." She cleared her throat.

"Wait!" Dobbs hung his head in defeat. "A'right. I'll take ya to 'im."

7

THE BELLA RAMONA

"What is that smell?" Imogen pinched her nose as we carefully stepped over a pile of horse manure in the road. "And how do people live in all this soot?"

Dobbs shrugged. "'S just London, innit? When's the last time you was 'ere?"

"I live here, remember?"

"Don't you never look out the winda?"

"Of course I look out the window. It's just... a lot cleaner where I live."

Imogen grimaced at some smoke stacks rising up on our right, churning out black clouds that circled the city's spires and church towers and sat stagnant, like a swamp in the sky. On the road, last night's snow had been all churned up by cartwheels so that nothing remained but muddy, smelly slush. And if that wasn't bad enough, Dobbs had led us to a dirty shipping yard littered with boxes, barrels, rat-chewed rope and termite-eaten old boats.

"Where exactly are we, Dobbs?" I questioned, starting to feel the slightest bit concerned that now at last he might be leading us to a den of thugs.

"Ain't you never been to King's Cross afore?" Dobbs sounded incredulous again.

Imogen squinted at the buildings as we picked our way through the shipping yard. "If this is King's Cross, where's the train station?"

In answer, a shrill whistle belted out of the nearby fog. The next second, a dim light shone through the mist, growing ever brighter until a great, black, roaring steam engine erupted into view. It chugged, picked up speed and soon disappeared again into the murky fog beyond.

"Station's that way." Dobbs pointed in the direction from which the train had come. "But we ain't goin' there. Our business is in the canal."

We followed along as Dobbs meandered through the crates, chains and other junkyard objects and brought us to a towpath along the canal. A dense blanket of mist lay over the water and patches of thick ice drifted on its sluggish current. Nothing else moved down stream except for a pair of ducks and the odd swan, but a number of river barges were moored along the canal's sides. Most looked abandoned, but one – a handsome, crimson one with gold trim – showed signs of life. Its chimney pipe smoked and the sound of violin music drifted from its one round window.

"That'll be the Cap'n." Dobbs nodded towards the barge with a look of apprehension. "'S not too late to turn back and call it a day," he added with a hint of hopefulness that struck me as suspicious.

I squinted at him. "You're not really frightened of this old bargeman person, are you? You just want us to forget this whole venture so you don't lose out."

Dobbs chewed his chapped bottom lip sheepishly but said nothing.

"Well, I hate to break it to you, but I'm not leaving here without those sketches. So stop being a scaredy cat and lead us to that boat," I added for good measure.

"Scaredy cat? Me?" Dobbs's face tensed up as if he were wrestling with himself until he exploded. "A'right, a'right. I admit it. I was just 'oping you'd change your mind about the sketchemy-fingy. I'll take you to 'im." He stepped down onto the icy towpath and spoke over his shoulder. "Mind you, the Cap'n ain't the jolliest chap as you're like to meet. Fact is, he's got the morbs. Keeps to 'imself mostly. But I reckon he's pretty well harmless." With that, Dobbs skipped and skidded along the towpath like a champion figure skater while Betsy did her best to stay at his heels while her elephant-like feet slid out from under her.

Imogen and I hung back as Dobbs approached the barge, removed his hat, rubbed down his shock of hair and rapped on the door with his raw, red knuckles.

Deafening barks answered from inside, muting the violin music. A second later, the door pushed open and a yapping black Labrador's slick head appeared. We couldn't see the bargeman, but we heard him shout from inside, "Stand down, Alpheus. It's only Dobbs, you half-crazed mongrel." The dog obediently tucked its head back inside. The voice spoke again. "I didn't expect to see you again so soon, Mr. Dobbs. What have you brought me this time?"

I had expected a different kind of voice from someone called "the old bargeman", harsher, gruffer. But from what I could hear, he spoke very correctly and softly.

"As it 'appens, Cap, I've brought along a couple o' ladies wot 'as got a matter o' business to discuss with yourself."

There was a pause.

"Ladies, you say? I'm not in the habit of entertaining ladies, but if it is genuinely a matter of business…"

Dobbs gave us a quick nod, then crossed a little plank of wood that served as a makeshift gangplank and disappeared inside the barge.

Imogen and I looked at each other.

"You sure about this?" she asked.

"I'm sure I have to get back those sketches."

She nodded.

I stepped first onto the slick plank of wood, bracing myself against the boat's side. Walking on an icy plank was ten times harder in Victorian boots and with a petticoat blocking the view of my next step.

I nearly lost my footing when, behind me, Imogen gasped. "Holy smokes! Katie, look."

She was staring at the barge where I'd just laid my hand. It was partly covering some words painted in gold cursive. I moved my hand away to read it: *Bella Ramona.*

My stomach lurched. *Ramona?* This was the last place I'd expected to see the name that had been turning over in my mind for months now. The very name I had been hoping to hear since we had arrived here in Victorian London. Could we really have stumbled upon a clue?

"You were right," Imogen said. "Seems the sketches *have* led us to the right place."

"We'll soon find out," I whispered. My spine tingled with excitement as I stepped down into the barge.

Inside, the air was close, warm and smelled of wood-fire smoke.

As my eyes adjusted to the dimness, a figure appeared in front of me, tall but stooped over due to the low ceiling. "There are seats by the fire. I'll put on the kettle," he said in the same soft voice.

Though my head could nearly have brushed the ceiling if I stood on tiptoe, the boat felt twice as big from the inside. A small foyer with hangers for hats and coats led to a cosy living room with a burning woodstove where the bargeman knelt over a copper kettle. Whatever lay beyond the main cabin – I guessed it was Captain Nemo's sleeping quarters – was hidden behind a curtain.

Small though the Captain's home was, every last bit of space – walls, ceiling and floor – displayed the oddest assortment of things: shelves lined with inkwells of every shape, a collection of Chinese fans displayed on the wall, figurine soldiers and antique maps, an easel in the corner with a half-finished painting.

Though my eyes wanted to carry on roving over all the eccentric bits and bobs, they kept returning to that unfinished painting of a girl in a simple, white dress standing in a grassy meadow. Only her back was visible, her long, black hair falling in waves to her waist. Her brown hands were lifted up to the sky, as if she were praying. My eyes wandered to a little desk beside the easel. There lay Ramona's sketches, all strewn about as if the bargeman had been looking through them.

"Shiver me timbers!"

I jumped, interrupted from my observations by a loud croaking voice and the sound of flapping wings.

"Walk the plank, scurvy dog!"

An enormous raven was swinging from a perch hung from a ceiling beam.

"Don't mind Billy Bones. Intelligent, but it seems he can't be taught manners," the bargeman said as he set a tray with mismatched tea mugs on an upturned crate beside the fire. It was not until he came towards me balancing a cup and saucer that I noticed the bargeman's right toes turned severely inwards causing him to walk with a limp. I smiled and took the cup, trying to act as though I hadn't observed the disability.

"Walk the plank, scurvy dog!" the raven squawked again.

The two dogs, stretched out happily in front of the wood stove, raised their heads. The Captain, however, ignored the insult and gestured to some stools placed around the tea things. He waited for the three of us to be seated, then limped over to a high-backed armchair, sat with a grunt of pain, then took a pipe from his waistcoat pocket and began filling it. I stole a glance at him over my tea mug as the embers lit up his dark face.

He was handsome, I thought, in a stern, pirate-like way. His hair, which had been dark but was greying at the temples, was pulled back into a ponytail. It was hard to tell his age through his thick black beard and heavy eyebrows, which hovered like two thunderclouds over stormy eyes.

What with the bad leg, the black beard and the burgundy handkerchief tied around his throat, I almost felt that we really were aboard a pirate ship, inside the captain's quarters. It was giving me a terribly hot, prickly feeling as I sat there stewing beside the wood stove.

The captain didn't speak for what felt like a long time. He just crossed his legs and smoked his pipe as if we weren't there at all. I wondered if perhaps he was waiting for us to speak, so I said the thing weighing on my mind. Clearing my throat, I casually observed, "It's an interesting name for a barge, *Bella Ramona*. Did you name it after someone in particular?"

He blew smoke from his nostrils. "Just had a nice ring to it is all. Better than, say, *Bella Bertha*." A very slight smile flickered on his lips and vanished.

Intuition told me he was concealing something. "Then… you don't know *anyone* by the name Ramona?"

His eyes narrowed. "What sort of business was it you wanted to discuss?"

Dobbs, who seemed even more fidgety and nervous than I felt, piped up. "It's a bit o' business, like I said, Cap'n. Regardin' that leather folder I sold ya last night."

"What about it?" the Captain grumbled impatiently.

Dobbs whistled, then laughed nervously, then actually seemed at a loss for words.

"The thing is," I started, still trying to sound casual,

"the sketchbook Dobbs sold you didn't actually belong to him. It belonged to me, and he..." I glanced at Dobbs who was chewing his bottom lip fiercely. "We had a bit of a... misunderstanding. I didn't *technically* give him permission to sell it. So, we've come to ask if we might... just... have it back... please?"

The bargeman leaned forward in his chair, fiddling with a gold ring on his little finger. "Well now, let's see. I paid good money for that leather, and how was I to know it wasn't lawfully acquired by Mr. Dobbs here? If I give it back, I lose out on business. Buying and trading, that's how I make my living, Miss..."

"Watson," I said.

"Well then, Miss Watson, you see my predicament." He never raised his voice, but something in his soft, persistent way of speaking made me horribly uneasy.

I swallowed, determined to stand my ground. "Then Dobbs will pay you back your money. Right Dobbs?"

Dobbs cast an anxious look from me to the bargeman and back. "Can't, Miss," he whispered.

"Why not?" I whispered back, though I was quite sure the bargeman could hear every word.

"'Cause... I spent it. Them apples an' things them bobbies was chasin' me for weren't stole. I bought 'em fair an' square."

"Except you didn't," Imogen said in a voice intended for all to hear. "You bought them with money you made selling stolen goods."

Dobbs raised his palms helplessly. "Sorry, Miss. Can't very well sell back them apples now, can I? Wot I 'adn't already et up or gave to Samson - ya know, my unfortunate mule friend – I dropped in the chase."

I could tell Imogen was only just restraining herself from putting Dobbs back into a chokehold. A lot of good that would do. It was clear Captain Nemo would not give in unless there was something in it for him. I looked down at the satchel in my lap. In it were most of my greatest treasures in the world: my detective notebook, Ramona's sketches (until Dobbs got his smudgy hands on them), and the Serpent Stone. The stone was a little piece of Cherokee Country, a reminder of Wattie, Ka-Ti, Jim and the others. But the sketches, they were more than just keepsakes. They were my connection to Ramona, my only hope of finding her. I knew what I had to do.

"Mr.... sorry, *Captain* Nemo, perhaps we can make a trade?"

He sat back and stroked his beard. "What did you have in mind?"

I opened my satchel, felt for the stone and lay it on my open palm for him to see.

Nemo leaned in closer, took one look and laughed. "A rock for a leather folder? Not really a fair trade, is it?"

"It isn't *just* a rock," I persisted. "It's a legendary Native American stone, supposed to possess great magic." The frown on his face made me regret mentioning the magic bit. "Well, anyway," I fumbled, "It's a unique artefact, so it must be worth more than an ordinary piece of leather."

Captain Nemo sat back and began to turn the ring 'round and 'round his finger again. "I might agree, Miss Watson. *If...*"

"*If* what?" Imogen asked impatiently.

He stopped turning the ring and wove his fingers together. "*If* it *were* just an ordinary piece of leather. But as it happens, that leather folder is full of rather extraordinary sketches, which makes me reckon there must be an extraordinary story as to how you came by it." He watched me intently.

This was my chance to watch him too, to find out what he wasn't telling us. "Those sketches belonged to a woman. A woman with the same name as your boat."

I saw his eyes flicker as I said it. "Are you sure you've never met anyone by that name?"

Every muscle in his face was tensed. I couldn't tell if it was anger or pain in the lines between his eyebrows, but his voice was stone cold. "What if I have? What's she to you?"

"She's... a relation," I answered, trying to keep the surge of excitement from gushing up into my voice. I had been right. The boat's name was no coincidence. He knew Ramona.

"A relation?" He looked at me suspiciously. "You don't look like her much."

And now he had just admitted it. "We're... cousins. Distant cousins. On my father's side." I couldn't stand it anymore. I had to ask. "Do you know where I can find her?"

His eyes fixed on mine for another second, then dropped. "I can't help you. I knew her once, but that was long, long ago. I've not seen her or heard of her since."

With that, he pushed himself out of his chair and reached for his walking cane. But as he stood, his eyes betrayed him, flickering momentarily towards the half-finished painting on the easel.

I was on my feet without realising it. "It's her, isn't it?"

He didn't turn around. "Like I said, it was long ago. Before she left."

Left? My heart did a somersault. "But when did she leave? And where did she go?"

The bargeman whirled around, his eyes flaming with anger. "I've told you, haven't I? I don't know. I can't help you. You want to know what became of her? Ask Phineas Webb." He turned his back to me again and braced himself on the little desk that held the scattered sketches.

It took a few trembling breaths before I could ask, "Who is Phineas Webb?"

It was Dobbs that answered. "Ah, come off it, Miss. You're 'aving a laugh! Who doesn't know the most famous painter in all of Britain? Maybe the whole world!"

Captain Nemo gave a mirthless laugh. "Yes, yes. A man of timeless genius! The most celebrated talent of our age!" His raised voice was as icy as the canal's waters, then it dropped and he mumbled to himself as he hobbled to the back of the boat. "His ship may have come in, but we have our barge. The River is our Kingdom. We may not live in halls of marble, but still we have some pretty ornaments… we have our freedom and our dignity. Two treasures he doesn't understand. Well, his day is coming. You can tell him that!"

He shouted the last bit at us, as if we were meant to deliver the message. Then he carried on mumbling to himself as he disappeared behind the curtain. Imogen was giving me a look that said, *"Let's get out of here quick."*

I had no doubt there was much more this Captain Nemo could tell us, but if I pushed him any further, it seemed he was likely to crack. I didn't fancy finding out just how mad he could get while we were stuck within the confines of his boat.

Hesitantly, I lay the serpent stone on the little desk – as much as it made me sick to part with it, I had made a offer to Nemo, and I was going to keep my part of it – then I stepped towards the closed curtain and cleared my throat. "Thank you, Captain. We should really be going…"

"Yea," Imogen echoed. "Now you've got that lovely snake stone to add to your collection, so why don't we just take these old sketches and leave you to enjoy your things…"

She had just gathered up the sketches and handed them to me when the curtain was whipped back. Captain Nemo loomed in the doorway. "I'm afraid that won't be possible," he said in his old, polite tone; but his eyes were wild.

I suddenly noticed the floor beneath my feet was rattling, as if the barge had come to life like a dragon woken from slumber. It sent a chill of panic up my spine that made me whirl around for the door.

Captain Nemo advanced, his eyes fixed on the sketchbook. "You see, Miss Watson," – He moved between me and the way out – "What's inside that book is worth a lot more to me than leather. I've waited a long, long time… I'm not about to let a treasure like that leave this barge."

My fingers tightened around the folder. "But we're not leaving without it."

"Then have a seat. It's going to be a long journey." He

pushed past me and threw back the curtain to reveal the part of the barge that had been hidden: an open door that led to an outer deck with a steering stick. Inside was a coal engine, and it was burning.

The Captain ducked out the door and hobbled up to the steering deck. He was visible from the waist down only, but I could see him manoeuvring the steering stick and felt the boat responding.

"Katie, look!" Imogen pointed to the small, round window. "We're moving down the canal."

Sure enough, we were drifting away from the mooring; slowly, yes, but once we reached the middle of the canal, there would be no getting off that boat.

"Now's our only chance to get out of here," I whispered to Imogen. "Quick, to the other door."

But before we could take a step, Captain Nemo returned to the cabin, a rope coiled over one shoulder.

"Dobbs, do me the favour of securing our friends here. I'll make it worth your while."

He tossed the rope to Dobbs who caught it in both hands. Now we were caught between a kidnapper and a crook. There was no way out.

Dobbs frowned at the rope in his hands for a moment then shook his head. "Can't 'elp you there, Cap'n."

"What do you mean?" Nemo hobbled over to him and seized the rope. "Man the aft, then. I'll do it myself."

That was when Arty Dobbs decided to play the hero instead of the crook. With one slick movement, he kicked the walking stick out of the bargeman's grip so that the man toppled over and crashed against the wall.

"Walk the plank, scurvy dog!" Billy Bones screeched as the Captain pushed himself up, cursing, only to take another tumble over Alpheus who had come to his master's aid and was worrying in circles at his feet.

"Wot are you waitin' for!" Dobbs waved us to follow him to the aft. "Let's split, afore we drifts any farther!"

We scrambled up onto the steering deck where Dobbs grasped the stick and pulled back hard. "Hoist that gangplank, 'n' quick!"

I found the plank of wood and slid it towards the bank. The end just reached, but we were still drifting, and angry, uneven footsteps were approaching from within the boat.

"Well don't just 'ang about, get goin'!"

Imogen scuttled across the moving gangplank; then it was my turn. "What about you and Besty?" I called to Dobb.

"Ah, that ol' blighter won't 'urt us." No sooner had he said it, the Captain's enraged face appeared in the doorway. He hobbled with amazing speed up onto the deck and grabbed Dobbs by the collar.

Before I could move, Betsy was there, her jaws locked on the Captain's trousers, tugging with all her bullish strength.

"Katie, hurry up, it's about to fall!" Imogen screeched from the towpath.

I turned back. The barge was drifting faster now, the gap widening by the second. With a gasp, I clutched the sketchbook and rushed across the gangplank, jumping onto solid ground just before the piece of wood plopped into the water.

A much louder splash followed.

"Oh no," I gasped, expecting to see Dobbs's top hat bobbing in the canal. Instead, Captain Nemo spluttered and flailed in the half-frozen water. He had pulled away from Betsy's iron jaws all right, but it had sent him over the rail and into the canal.

Dobbs cast him a rope, then called over his shoulder at us, "Don't worry! Bess & me'll see he don't drown. Now run for it!"

Imogen ran on, but I hesitated.

"Come on, Katie," she urged. "You heard him."

I didn't feel right abandoning Dobbs. He had the upper hand now, but would Nemo try to kill him after the boy reeled him back to safety? Dobbs seemed confident he wouldn't, and besides, the man would be too cold and weary to catch a slick squirrel like Dobbs. Reassured, I turned and sped after Imogen, the excitement of our escape making me reckless as I pulled up my skirt and jumped over bits of scrap in the shipping yard. I didn't even notice the pile of horse manure until my foot landed in it. I slid before falling hard on my tailbone. The sketchbook flew out of my grasp; the sketches went everywhere.

Seeing stars from the pain, I turned over onto my knees and started gathering the sketches as quickly as I could.

"Are you all right?" Imogen had run back to help me.

"Fine," I winced. "I just don't want to lose a single…" My hand landed on a piece of parchment – the sketch of the old woman at St. Paul's – and froze. Pinning a corner of the parchment to the ground was the toe of a large, shiny black shoe. My eyes travelled slowly upward, finally coming to land on the face of Detective-Inspector Sherringdon Janklow.

As he peered down his beak-like nose at me, one of his eyebrows rose high above the other. "How nice to see you again, Miss Watson. I dare to say a little chat is in order. Wouldn't you agree?"

8

A REASONABLE CONCLUSION

We rattled along the mist-shrouded, cobbled streets of London in a hansom cab. Glancing out the window, I could just make out the silhouettes of lamplighters climbing up and down their ladders. My stomach grumbled, forcing me to acknowledge just how weary and hungry and anxious I felt. Inspector Janklow had shown us nothing but kindness; he had helped us gather up the scattered sketches and had called the cab to take us back to his office in Lincoln's Inn Fields. But what he intended to do with the sketches, or with us, once we got there... We could only wait and find out.

"We'll save the questions for a nice hot fire and a steaming cup of mulled wine, shall we?" he had said as he helped Imogen and me into the cab. "It's best not to say anything *off the record*, if you gather my meaning."

And so no one spoke a word for the whole journey. I watched the busy streets go by out the window and exchanged a few glances with Imogen. She looked flushed and tired and as uncertain as I felt. What were we in for at the end of this journey? Would the sketch be enough to convict us of having a hand in the case of the stolen St. Paul's painting?

I rubbed my hands together in my lap and took a deep breath. *You're not guilty, Katie, so don't act as if you are. Just tell the truth... or, at least, part of it.*

The only trouble was, the truth was hardly believable to a sensible, serious sort of man like this Inspector Janklow. It might save us from prison only to get us thrown into an insane asylum. How would we convince him we were both innocent *and* sane?

The cab pulled up to a two-storey building that leaned so badly to one side, it looked like it might lose its balance and collapse at any moment.

At the door, which tilted at the same angle as the building, Inspector Janklow took a large ring of keys from his coat pocket and fished for the one he wanted. He unlocked the wonky door and held it open to us with a kind, reassuring smile, as if we were his welcome guests; yet I couldn't help wondering whether we were being lured into a web we wouldn't easily get out of.

The building was abandoned and dark, but the Inspector lit a few lamps; then, taking a candle, led us up a narrow, slanted staircase and into a small, slanted office. To my surprise, lopsided walls aside, the room was a picture of orderliness.

The Inspector politely took our shawls and invited us to sit in two chairs before a big, mahogany desk while he started a fire. I looked over the desk. Its surface was spotlessly clean, arranged with a tidy stack of papers framed by a magnifying glass, a ruler and a row of quills organised by size. All this was watched over by a marble bust with the name Aristotle carved at the base.

"Now," said the Inspector, rising from the fire and brushing off his knees, "A little festive tipple to warm us up, eh?" He poured us each a small glass of mulled wine and took his seat across from us at the immaculate desk.

Inspector Janklow sipped his wine, straightened a quill on the desk that already looked perfectly straight to me, then leaned forward on his elbows, his fingertips touching to form a steeple that framed his beak-like nose. His mouth drew a straight line, pursed in thought. I could almost see the cogs turning in his head as his squinted eyes shifted mechanically between Imogen and me, like a pendulum.

I took a tiny sip from my glass and looked down at my lap where the sketchbook rested, a little wet but all intact, thank goodness.

"Miss Watson and Miss Humphreys... I have got that right, haven't I?"

I looked up and nodded, amazed that he remembered our names from our brief encounter the night before. "Yes, sir."

He nodded once. "And you know who I am, so let's get straight to the point, shall we? Twice now I have had the pleasure of meeting you young ladies, on both occasions without guardian or chaperone. Do you wish to explain these extraordinary circumstances to me?"

Imogen and I glanced at one another; then, to my relief, she spoke. "My parents had to leave suddenly to look after an elderly, infirm uncle in... um... County Durham."

The Inspector's one eyebrow rose. "And they didn't leave you in the care of a guardian?"

"Oh, um, yes. Of course. They left us with my old aunt. But she's also very infirm and never leaves the house."

He looked deeply perplexed now. "But surely your parents would not permit you to wander the city's streets without a governess or chaperone?"

"Oh, I've never had either. My parents believe girls ought to learn to be independent. It's a dangerous world out there, Inspector. We must all be on our guards."

Imogen really is a marvellous actress, I thought in admiration.

The Inspector sat back and retreated into his thoughts. "Humphreys... Humphreys..." he said to himself as if trying to recall something. "I don't suppose you're descended from *the* Duke Humphreys?"

Imogen's mouth hovered open for a second. "Yes!" she blurted. "Yes, I am. Great-great grandfather Humphreys. That's the one."

The Inspector nodded and lay his finger aside his nose. "That explains something. Always were an eccentric family, but then these old families often are. Still, if I were your father, Miss, I'd advise you to exercise your independence in a more savoury part of town than King's Cross wharf."

Imogen nodded modestly. "Yes, sir."

The Inspector brought his fingertips together again. "The question begs, nonetheless, *why* you found yourselves in that part of town this afternoon." Now he turned to me for an answer.

Just tell the truth, Katie. I thought. *There's nothing wrong with the truth.* "We went to get back my sketchbook from someone who had taken it."

"Ah, your sketchbook." He raised his pointer finger. "And now we come to it. Might I have another look at that particular sketch, Miss Watson? I'm sure you know which I mean."

With a gulp, I took the sketch of the old woman and the girl at St. Paul's from the top of the pile and passed it to him across the desk.

He squared its edges up perfectly with his other documents, then reached for the magnifying glass. Leaning over the sketch, he swept over every magnified bit of it.

Finally, he sat up and returned the glass to its proper place on the desk before resuming his calm posture. "Almost an exact replica of the painting that mysteriously appeared in St. Paul's Cathedral just last night ... a painting not even the most knowledgeable art critics seem to know anything about... the very painting that replaced the stolen masterpiece, *The Wedding Feast*." He paused and gave me a hard look. "Did you make this sketch, Miss Watson?"

"I... no sir! It was given to me. The entire collection of sketches was a gift."

"From whom, may I ask?"

I was trying desperately to think how to answer in a way that wouldn't sound insane, but the longer I put off answering, the guiltier I would appear. "It belongs to a woman called Ramona," I said in a rush. "I've never met her, but she's a relative of mine. I'm trying to find her."

"You don't know where she lives?"

"No, sir. She's been missing for some time. None of the

family knows where she's gone, but we think she may be here in London, because... well, because of this." I indicated the sketch. "But we promise we were telling you the truth last night. We don't know anything about that stolen painting."

"It's true," Imogen chimed in. "We just wanted to find Ramona."

"A missing person. Why didn't you come out and say so sooner?" Inspector Janklow frowned and tapped his finger against the side of his nose, deep in thought.

"Do you think..." I hesitated, not wanting to interrupt what was probably an ingenious train of thought.

"Go on, Miss Watson."

"I was just wondering if perhaps the two cases might be related? I mean, maybe if we find who stole the painting, they might lead us to Ramona?"

"Or the other way 'round?" He gave me a shrewd sideways look. "What sort of woman is this relative of yours?"

"Oh, she's not a criminal," I answered hastily. I leafed through the sketches and found one of Ramona in a forest clearing, lifting a baby Ka-Ti up over her head and laughing. "That's her there, with her daughter."

The Inspector looked at it thoughtfully. "And have you any notion of who might be behind her disappearance? Did she have relations in London? Friends?" His voice deepened as he said, "Enemies?"

"Well..."

I looked at Imogen. She was looking back at me as if unsure whether she ought to say any more.

"Go on, Miss Humphreys."

"We met someone today," she said. "Calls himself

'Captain Nemo', owns a boat called 'Ramona' and would do anything to get his hands on these sketches."

"Go on."

"He runs some kind of pawn shop on a barge…"

The Inspector listened intently as Imogen related our strange encounter with the old bargeman and our narrow escape. "That's why we were in the wharf this afternoon, and why we were running when we… well… ran into you."

He was nodding by the time she finished. I felt my chest ease up a little. It seemed Inspector Janklow believed our story entirely now. He even looked impressed by our daring getaway from the bargeman, though Imogen hadn't given fair credit to Dobbs for his part.

Seized by a sudden idea, I broke in. "Inspector Janklow, do you think we might be able to… that is, I don't know if you ever… I just thought…"

He listened patiently to my drivel. "Go on, Miss Watson. What was it you thought?"

Why was I so nervous? I took a deep breath and tried again. "Do you think we could help you solve the case?" Before he could answer, I quickly added, "Because we've had some practice in solving mysteries, and I really believe we could learn a lot from you, and maybe even be of some assistance."

What was his expression? Doubt? Or worse, amusement? I felt my cheeks flush.

"A detective's work is, by nature, solitary, Miss Watson."

How ridiculous he must have thought I was. *Me* offering to help *him*.

"But…"

I looked up at this hopeful word, 'but'.

"There is merit in what you suggest, and no man is ever really an island. My web of informants spreads into every nook and cranny of this city, from the highest to the very meanest. A detective, you see, must have eyes everywhere. And I am, in fact, in the habit of employing young people. Children, I find, often offer the most perceptive observations of society that we rusty old know-it-alls are all too prone to miss. But…" His expression changed suddenly; it reminded me of the look my dad gives when he's lecturing Charlie and me about something important, like what to do if you meet a bear in the woods. Instinctively, I sat up a little straighter. "*If* I were to take on an apprentice or say, two apprentices, well then I would have to know that they were *entirely trustworthy*." The eyes ticktocked between us again before he continued. "And trust must be earned through trial. I hope you don't think me indelicate."

"Uh, no, sir," we both answered, unsure of what exactly we were being put up to.

"And so," he continued, "I shall consider your proposal over Christmas supper."

I blinked. An invitation to Christmas supper was not what I had expected, but I felt an enormous weight lift off my shoulders.

Meanwhile, at the word 'supper', Imogen's stomach made an enormously loud grumble.

"Good grief!" She said, hugging her middle, "I completely forgot it's still Christmas!"

Inspector Janklow handed me back the sketch, straightened his desk, then got up and walked around to a coat rack. He took his cape, slung it around his shoulders, then offered us our shawls. "I'm sure Mrs. Janklow would be glad of some female company if your aunt can spare you and if you would care to join us?"

Imogen and I looked at each other, unable to hide the smiles spreading across our faces. Now my stomach joined in with the hungry chorus.

"We dine modestly, mind you. Perhaps not up to the standards to which you're accustomed, Miss Humphreys."

"Don't worry," Imogen said, slinging her shawl over her shoulders. "*This* Humphreys eats just about anything."

9

CHRISTMAS WITH THE JANKLOWS

"*B*less my soul! And nowhere to go for Christmas dinner?" Mrs. Janklow exclaimed for at least the twelfth time. Again she shook her head, clasped her hands over her heart and added, "Oh, I thank the heavens Sherry found you when he did. It isn't worth *thinking* what might have happened." Then, after wiping her eye with the corner of her apron, "More potatoes, my dears?"

Inspector Janklow's home was only a short walk north from his office. It was a snug little brick house sandwiched between identical snug brick houses on Bedford Row. There was a homemade Christmas wreath on the cherry red door and the smell of a wonderful, hot roast to greet us on the other side.

Mrs. Janklow had fluctuated between tears of ecstasy and tears of concern from the moment she laid eyes on us and Inspector Janklow explained how he had discovered us all alone in King's Cross. She had taken us in like a mother hen gathering chicks, and hadn't stopped feeding and fussing over us the whole evening.

"What courageous little souls you are," she said, helping us both to another slice of roast goose. "To go out looking for that missing woman all on your own. Why, it reminds me of that Miss Gladden, the young lady detective from the gazette."

"Actually," I said, swallowing a bite of hot chestnut stuffing, "We're in training to be detectives. We were hoping to learn a few things from your husband. That is, if he decides to let us help him on the case." I cast a quick glance at the Inspector who was gnawing on his pipe by the fire. He seemed far away in his own thoughts.

Mrs. Janklow gave her husband a shrewd look. "Oh yes, Sherry, what an excellent idea," she said, though he hardly seemed to hear her. "Why there's no one better to learn from. Sherry is as cunning as a dockyard fox!" Her smooth, rosy cheeks glowed with pride.

Mrs. Janklow had just served the Christmas pudding when there came a knock at the door. Inspector Janklow went into the hallway to answer it and quickly returned. "Constable Smart requires my assistance identifying a suspect. I won't be any longer than is necessary, my dear. These young ladies will keep you company, I am sure." He threw on his overcoat, picked up his bowler hat and walking stick from the corner, kissed his wife and was gone.

Mrs. Janklow smiled cheerfully as she poured brandy butter over our Christmas pudding, but she let a sigh escape as she sat down to eat her own.

"Does the Inspector ever get a day off?" I asked.

She smiled sweetly but sadly. "Matters of justice never can wait ... not even on Christmas." She sighed again. "Being a detective is a noble calling, but it does have its sacrifices. Family life, for one. I always wanted children." Though she never stopped smiling, her eyes misted over. "I had a little boy once, but he died an infant. Thought it would break my poor husband's heart. He's not been the same ever since. Pours himself, heart and soul, into his work now. I suppose he reckons if he can't have a child of his own, at least he can make this old world safer for other people's children."

Mrs. Janklow wiped her now fast-falling tears on her apron. She looked younger than her husband with soft skin and rich black curls, and seemed perfectly cut out for motherhood. I tried to imagine the Inspector, so somber and tidy and correct, with a drooling baby on his knee. I wondered if he would look younger and happier, and wear less black if his son had lived.

Mrs. Janklow blew her nose, then swiftly brushed away the cloud hanging over her and smiled brightly. "Ah, but isn't the good Lord kind, sending us two such lovely young ladies to brighten up this old house on Christmas? You're just like Spring sunshine, you are."

Despite her protests, we did our best to help Mrs. Janklow wash up the dinner things. Then, we all sat by the hearth in the Janklows' clean, cosy parlour. She let Imogen and me roast a basket of chestnuts over the fire while she perched on a nearby workbench, picked up a basket of cross-stitching and started to work on a handkerchief.

I admired how nimbly she stitched the intricate pattern of an ivy vine. "I was learning to cross-stitch a while ago,"

I said, remembering fondly how Sophia had tried to teach me at Otterly Manor. "But I was never much good at it."

"Ah, well, all it takes is a bit of practice, and I'm sure you'd be as quick with a needle as any." She patted the seat of her work bench. "Come, I've got some extra screens. Why not give it another try now?"

Timidly, I accepted the fabric, needle and thread and took a seat beside her.

"It's like this. That's it. It'll become second nature in no time." She continued to praise and encourage my efforts while I watched and copied her movements. As I got better at stitching, Mrs. Janklow asked me about my family, and before I knew it, we were chatting away like old friends. I told her about my parents and Charlie, and how he always played detective games with me when he lived at home.

"I guess that's what first got me thinking about becoming a *real* detective," I told her.

"And what is it about being a *real* detective that excites you?"

No one had ever asked me that before. I thought a moment before answering. "I like helping people out of their troubles. Same as your husband, I guess."

She stopped stitching and gave me a long, approving look.

Just then, the door opened and Inspector Janklow stood in the parlour doorway, brushing snow off his shoulder. I could hardly believe he was back already. The evening had passed so pleasantly and quickly in Mrs. Janklow's company.

"I've called a cab for you as it's late," he said. "Waiting

outside when you're ready."

"Oh, must they go, Sherry?" Mrs. Janklow protested. "I could fix up Jonathan's... I mean, the spare room for them."

He kissed her bowed head and patted her hand. "My dear, these girls are not pets. They have homes of their own."

We thanked a teary Mrs. Janklow over and over as we bundled up, then left the house with little sacks full of hot chestnuts for the journey. I was grateful for such kind hospitality, but I couldn't help feeling let down. Inspector Janklow was clearly eager to see us on our way. I was sure he had decided he did not need a couple of girls getting in the way of his important work. We were on our own.

But when we reached the cab door, instead of opening it, he turned to face us. "I never make an important decision without consulting the Missus. Without meaning to boast, she is a keen one and an impeccable judge of character, understand?"

I nodded, not sure what all this meant.

He held the cab door open and, as we were about to climb in, said, "Meet me tomorrow outside Jamaica Coffee House in Covent Garden Market, nine a.m., to discuss the stipulations of our partnership."

I stared blankly, hardly believing my ears. We both shook hands with him and wished him a Merry Christmas. The carriage had left Bedford Row behind before it hit me what had happened. We were going to partner with a real, London detective! The tiny flicker of hope that we might actually find Ramona in this monstrous maze of a city swelled into a glowing flame.

10

ON THE CASE

Next morning, we found Dobbs and Betsy approaching the iron gate of the Misses Turveys' Hostel for Girls of Good Character.

"Mornin' me 'arties," he said cheerfully, falling in beside us as we joined the bustling traffic in the street.

"What happened after we left?" I asked him as we turned down Long Acre street towards Covent Garden Market.

Dobbs shrugged. "I 'elped Nemo back into the barge, got 'im a cup o' tea. Then he moored up and Betsy 'n' me went on our way."

Imogen's eyes widened. "You mean he just let you go? Just like that?"

Dobbs gave a look that said, *well obviously*. "Didn't 'ave any beef with me, did he? It was you 'n' that sketchbook o' yours 'e was after. Makes a fella wonder..." He stopped in his tracks, turned to face us and leaned against the wall as if to say he wasn't going a step further until we coughed up some information. "Come out with it, then. What's so special 'bout them sketches. Who's this Ramona bird you're on the hunt for?"

Imogen and I looked at each other with uncertainty, but neither of us said a word.

"Ah, come on. You can tell us," Dobbs said, straightening his tattered collar with an air of respectability. "I did truly 'elp you out of a fix yesterday. Ain't we even yet?"

Imogen huffed. I bit my lip.

"I coulda tied you up like Nemo said, an' been paid a pretty sum for it, but I risked me own neck instead…" He looked desperate. "I'd just like to know what it's all about, 's all. Maybe I can 'elp. If you're lookin' for somebody as is missing, why there's none better 'n me to 'elp you. I know every crook 'n' nanny o' this ol' city, I do. You can count on me. I never chirp on me friends."

Friends, he'd said. Were we friends with Arty Dobbs, the petty criminal and prince of the street Arabs? I looked into his enormous, hungry green eyes and felt that *this* time, he was telling the truth. Maybe those had been his true colours he'd shown when he risked his own neck to help us escape yesterday, like the time he'd rescued Betsy. Maybe there really was a good heart in that dirty wrapping somewhere that just wanted a chance to shine. *And,* I thought, *it was Dobbs who led us to the Bella Ramona. Who knows? He might just prove himself valuable again.*

"All right," I said at last. "We'll let you in on our mission, but right now we're late for a meeting."

"Right-o." Dobbs blew into his fingerless gloves and rubbed his hands together. "Where to and who are we meeting?"

"Inspector Janklow at the Jamaica Coffee House."

Dobbs stopped again in his tracks with a groan. "Wot, a policeman? You're 'aving me on!"

"No, we're not," I assured him. "He's working on the case of the missing painting at St. Paul's, and we're going to help him. We think it might be connected to the woman we're looking for. To Ramona."

Dobbs shook his head. "I'll take you to the place, then wait outside for you. I might be reformin' my ways a little, but I ain't ready to frat'nise with the enemy as yet."

Imogen rolled her eyes. "A detective isn't technically a policeman, you know. But suit yourself. It's not as if you were invited anyway."

DOBBS LED us past the busy arcades of Covent Garden Market to the coffee house, then, slick as a squirrel, dodged carts and cabs to cross the road where he'd spotted a fellow street Arab (a tall, lean boy who appeared to be wearing more dirt than clothes).

The windows of the Jamaica Coffee House were too steamed up to see through. A bell over the door jingled as we pushed it open. The shop was hot and cramped with tables, but the customers looked much more elegant and friendly than those at Ye Olde Cheddar Cheese. No one stared as we wound our way through the tables, finally spotting a black-clad figure alone in the back corner, his face concealed by an open newspaper.

The Inspector rose to greet us, poured us each some coffee and offered a plate of cream buns before diving into the business of our meeting.

"I understand from what you've said that you ladies have some little practice in solving puzzles?"

"Yes, sir. Well, we've helped solve a mystery or two. And I've read lots of detective novels," I added a little shyly.

He took a long breath through his nostrils and lightly touched his fingertips together, just as he had in his office the day before. "Yes. I see. Solving a *real* crime, Miss Watson, is rather different to what you might have read in sensationalist detective novels or the penny dreadful. If we are to ... cooperate in this operation, I must ask you to comply with my methods." He raised his eyebrows meaningfully.

I felt he was waiting for me to ask for an explanation. "Of course," I said. "Could you perhaps review your methods ... just to be sure we're clear on them?"

He nodded. "In a phrase? The scientific method of deduction."

Imogen lowered her coffee cup. "You mean like observing facts, writing them down and then drawing the conclusions that fit best? Oh, Katie's brilliant at that. She's *always* writing little details down in her detective notebook she carries with her everywhere."

"I believe you have the general idea, Miss Humphreys. It's like I always say." He tapped his finger against his temple. "A mystery is only as thick as the man's head who's trying to solve it. Anything can be explained by cold, hard Reason."

How about magic? I wanted to ask. But instead, I said, "But Inspector Janklow, just supposing there *was* something *really* mysterious going on. Shouldn't we at least keep our minds open to the possibility?"

He said nothing, but drew a gold pocketwatch from his waistcoat pocket and rested it in his open palm for us to see. "Every case is like this pocketwatch, Miss Watson. All the cogs and wheels must be fitted together, and it all starts ticking, like clockwork. When Reason unveils the thing, it will prove to be no more mysterious than the movement of this clock's hands, mark my words." This time he thumped the side of his nose. "I'll winkle it out if Reason can do it, and Reason never fails to do it." He returned the watch to his pocket. "Now, I must have your faith in my methods if a partnership is to be established. Do I have your confidence and cooperation?"

In my own mind, I hesitated. It was only a second, but I felt the Inspector's sharp eyes watching, so I nodded. But something like guilt was nibbling away at my stomach. There was simply no getting around the fact that this *was* a mysterious case, that Reason alone would never solve it. But what could I do? Janklow spoke of Reason like it was a father figure. If I told him the things we'd seen and done that defied Reason, he would never believe them. And we needed him on our side.

It's not being dishonest, I reassured myself. *It's just agreeing to let him do things his way and not interfere.* He was still looking at me keenly, so I cleared my throat and said earnestly, "We'll do our best, sir."

"Much obliged," he said with a business-like smile. "Now that's in order, how will our agreement play out? Here's my thinking." He outlined a plan in which we would conduct our investigations separately, then meet and compare notes. "We can cover more ground that way, and it will be easier to move about unnoticed if we are not always travelling in caravan."

We agreed with him.

"Though I would like you to join me at the scene of the crime. I've arranged to meet an art dealer contact of mine and some of the clergy of St. Paul's in two days' time. Meanwhile, I shall dig around to see what I can discover about this Captain Nemo, and I suggest the two of you spend some time with this." He reached into a leather case at his feet and pulled out a large paper envelope with the stamped words *Metropolitan Police, Case File*. "Guard it safely, and only remove its contents in private."

I took it from him carefully, but inside felt a thrill of curiosity. "Is this evidence?" I asked, trying to sound business-like and not giddy with excitement. I thought perhaps taking a nonchalant sip of my coffee would help.

"Records," he answered. "Newspaper articles, photographs and critiques all surrounding the life and career of Mr. Webb."

A half-second earlier, and the sip of coffee would have spewed out of my mouth. I choked on it, but managed to swallow. "Did you say Mr. Webb?"

Inspector Janklow's sharp eyes travelled between my surprised face to Imogen's.

"That's right. Mr. Phineas Warwick Webb, my client." He tilted his head inquisitively. "You *did* know the stolen painting, *The Wedding Feast*, the most celebrated work of art of the last century, was painted by Mr. Webb... did you not?"

"Nn...no. We didn't." My heart was pumping so hard, I hardly managed to get the words out.

His eyebrows raised in surprise. "I do apologise. My mistake for assuming you were familiar with the details of the crime known to the general public."

"It's our fault," I said hastily. "We should read the newspaper more."

Imogen, still puzzled, asked, "Phineas Webb, wasn't he...?"

"Yes, Miss Humphreys?"

I answered for her. "Captain Nemo told us that if we wanted to know what had happened to Ramona, we should ask Phineas Webb."

At that, Inspector Janklow's deep frown lines appeared and his eyes got that far-off-in-thought look again. "Hmmm. Another point of connection," he muttered to himself. "The missing painting, the missing woman... this Captain Nemo." He screwed up his face tighter, as if willing the answer to come to him. Then, "Nothing." His face relaxed. "But time, information and Reason must do their dance."

"Inspector, shouldn't we question Mr. Webb? I mean, he *must* have something to do with it all."

"He has a great deal to do with it all, Miss Watson. He is, as I say, my client, and most eager to recover his painting. We could hardly suspect the man of having nicked his own painting."

"No. I suppose not," I agreed, feeling a little humiliated. "But still, he might know something about Ramona. We could ask..."

"I understand your eagerness to follow this lead, Miss

Watson. But Mr. Webb is a very private man. One of those Bohemian-hermit-artist types. He is also a man of great wealth and power. If I go questioning him about a missing person, it could muddy the waters of the case, you understand."

I nodded.

"Perhaps one of my contacts in the art world will have some information."

"Couldn't *we* ask him about her?" Imogen asked. "I mean, not as detectives. Just as… you know… Fans."

To my surprise, Inspector Janklow actually seemed to consider this suggestion. "If you were to find a, shall we say, 'off-the-books' way of questioning Mr. Webb, I could not prevent you."

Imogen's eyes sparkled with excitement. "We'll think of a way," she said.

"The less I know, the better," the Inspector said. "So long as it's within the parameters of the law…" He gave us both a warning glare, then dabbed his mouth on the tablecloth and stood. "As it happens, I have my own curiosities about Phineas Webb. I'm not at liberty to snoop, professionally, but there are a great many things I'd like to know."

"We'll tell you what we find out," Imogen said, standing and brushing off her skirt. "And don't worry. We won't do anything illegal."

He raised an eyebrow. "Just one more word of advice, off the books as it were. I wouldn't ask Mr. Webb too direct or personal a question. As I've said, he is a *very* private gentleman. If he feels he's being pressed for information, I suspect he shall become an oyster and clam up, if you understand me."

THE STIFF, cold air hit me like a brick wall as we stepped outside. "Thank you for the coffee, Inspector." I said through my chattering teeth.

He nodded, his face furrowed in a concerned grimace as he tugged on his black leather gloves. "There is just one other thing, Miss Watson. Miss Humphreys. I hope you won't take this as a slight, but I really do feel it would be best if you had someone to accompany you."

Imogen looked like she was about to protest, but Janklow raised a hand and continued.

"However independent you may be, Miss Humphreys – and I am quite confident that you are – two young gentle ladies are sure to attract attention pottering about town on their own, and attention is the last thing we detectives want, you understand me?"

We both nodded reluctantly, neither of us sure of where this talk was going.

"What we need," Janklow continued, "is someone to play the part of chaperone. Someone we can trust, yes. But preferably someone who knows their way about town and who isn't afraid to throw punches when necessary."

An idea popped into my head, and from the look in Imogen's eye, I was sure she was thinking the same thing.

I glanced across the street and spotted a tall top hat braced on a pair of sticking-out ears and smiled. "Inspector, we know just the person."

11

THE AGE OF CHIVALRY

*I*nspector Janklow and Arty Dobbs stood face to face, as opposite as two people could be: the spotless inspector, propped elegantly against his walking cane, and the ragamuffin youngster, arms crossed over his chest and one suspicious, squinting eye. We had introduced them to one another and explained the Inspector's proposition to Dobbs, but it was far from a sealed deal yet.

"Haven't I seen you before, young man?" Janklow asked.

"Dunno, gov'nor. S'pose it's possible. I prefer to stay on the move."

"To steer clear of the constable, no doubt…"

Dobbs squinted the other eye. "You sure you ain't workin' for the constable yourself, gov?"

"You have my word," Janklow said, laying his gloved hand on his heart. "I work *with* the constable. I do not work *for* him." His eyebrow arched. "And what about yourself, Mr. Dobbs? Can I take you at your word that you are a man to be trusted?"

Dobbs's eyes dropped as he kicked the slushy ground with the missing toe of his shoe. He thought a moment, then looked up resolutely. "To those what know me, gov, to me friends, I'm as true as ol' Betsy."

Janklow cocked his head. "Old Betsy?"

"That's me dog." Dobbs whistled. At once, the bulldog left the overturned barrel of rubbish where she had been scavenging and came bounding up as in slow motion, jowls flapping like sails on a ship. This time, she didn't stop at her master's heels, but leapt up to greet Inspector Janklow, leaving two massive muddy paw stains on his pristine, crisp trousers.

I held my breath as the Inspector looked down at his spoiled trousers, sure that this was the end of our proposition. But he said nothing, only took a crisp, white handkerchief from his pocket and dotted the paw stains, which made no difference whatsoever. Then he stood upright, sniffed, and, to my relief, made a noble attempt at a smile. He carried on as if the attack on his cleanliness never happened.

"These young ladies tell me you know the city well. Is that so?"

"Chimneys to rat 'oles, gov." Dobbs puffed out his chest. "I know it all."

"Well, Mr. Dobbs. You might just prove to be the man for the job. Consider yourself and your mongrel on a probationary period. If you follow my instructions and do your job well, there'll be profit in it for you. If you prove untrustworthy, I cannot promise that the constable won't hear of it. That's the arrangement. Are you prepared to shake on it?" He held out his black-leathered hand.

Dobbs's ears were all aglow, and a jack-o-lantern grin was spreading across his face. "I am, gov!" In a flush of excitement, he spat into his own filthy hand and thrust it into the Inspector's, giving it a solid yank up and down.

Imogen and I watched, half in horror, half ready to explode with laughter. The Inspector grimaced, but shook Dobbs's hand with good grace; though, once the boy released it, I couldn't help noticing how he carefully held it behind his back and used his other hand to reach into his coat pocket. Drawing out a card, he handed it to Dobbs.

"Come to my office tomorrow midday, lad, and we'll discuss your duties."

Dobbs looked warily at the card. "You swear as there won't be any bobbies 'bout the place?"

"Not on my invitation. Between you and me," – the Inspector cupped his clean hand to his mouth – "I find the 'bobbies' just about as much a nuisance to my line of work as you do to yours. We may have more in common than you think, Mr. Dobbs."

With that, he nodded, took his walking stick under his arm and walked purposefully away down the market arcade while the three of us watched his retreat in admiration.

Dobbs made a low whistle. "I never thought as I'd see the day I'd be workin' for a detective." He thrust his thumb into his chest. "Inspector's assistant Arty Dobbs, tha's me!"

"Pipe down, would you?" Imogen muttered. "Don't you know anything about detective work? You're supposed to be stealthy."

Dobbs sneered. "Madame, *stealth* is me middle name.

So," he rubbed his hands together. "I'm to be your chaperone. Where d'ya want to go first?"

"Know where we can find Phineas Webb?" I asked.

"Wot, *the* Phineas Webb?"

I nodded. "Don't suppose you know where he lives?"

Dobbs gave another low whistle. "Dash it if I know where he lives. Don't often sally to those parts of town."

Imogen sighed. "Great start," she said sarcastically.

"But, as it 'appens, I do know where you can find him."

We looked at each other, then at Dobbs in amazement.

He grinned smugly. "Right this way, if you please, me ladies."

Dobbs led us down from Covent Garden Market to the Strand, the bustling thoroughfare that runs from Fleet Street all the way to Trafalgar Square. We, like Betsy, stayed close on his heels as he made his usual nimble way across the steady flow of omnibuses and cabs, towards a grand, triple-arched carriageway on the other side.

"This is Somerset House!" Imogen exclaimed as we passed beneath the arches and into a wide cobbled courtyard. "We've just been ice skating here."

Dobbs gave her a withering look. "No offence, miss, but you're off your rocker, you are. Right this way now."

He followed the outside of the courtyard to the right, where a line of men and women in furs and tall, feathered hats were entering one by one through a doorway. Over the door hung a gold-lettered sign that read *Exhibition Room*.

Several people made scandalised faces as Dobbs and

Betsy broke through their line, and one woman in a peacock hat held her handkerchief to her nose. We followed apologetically and joined him at the wall on the other side. He stood in front of a poster. As tall as a picture window, it featured an engraving of a black-haired maiden taking a rose from a horse-mounted knight. A garland of rose vines and exotic birds bordered the couple. An advertisement was printed below:

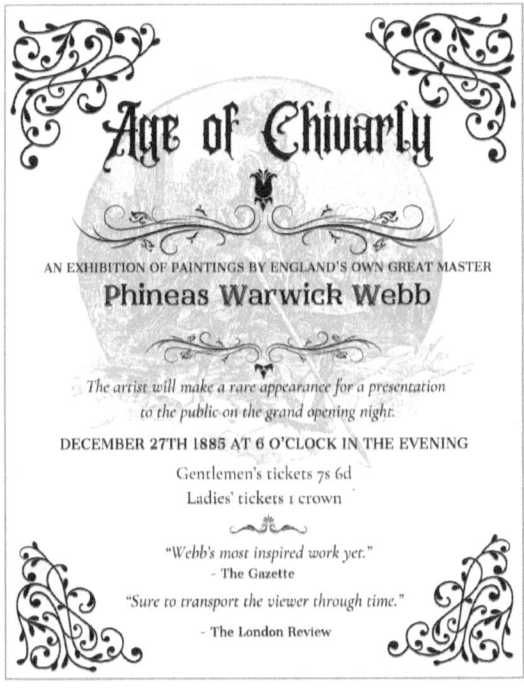

Imogen elbowed me. She was making eyes at the reviews in printed at the bottom of the poster. "You don't think it's serious?" she whispered.

I shook my head. "Just a figure of speech, I bet," I

answered under my breath. "But either way, we've got to go to that presentation tomorrow night."

"And where are we supposed to get the money for tickets?" We both thought a moment before Imogen added, "How much is that in modern money anyway?"

I looked to Dobbs who was leaning against the wall picking the dirt from his fingernails.

"Hey, Dobbs–"

He raised his head.

"How long would it take someone to earn, say, a crown or two?"

Dobbs whistled and shook his head. "Dash it if I know, Miss Katie. I've never touched a crown in me life."

Imogen threw her hands up with a disparaging "Oh great."

"But…" Dobbs rubbed his grubby fingers together. "Give me an afternoon 'n' I might just be able to line me pockets with a crown or two."

"Dobbs," I said in my firmest tone, "if you want to be our chaperone, you can *not* go picking any pockets, got it?"

He made a gentlemanly bow to show his acquiescence. "I'm at your command, me lady." He rubbed his freckled nose. "So how d'ya suggest we get the gold, eh?"

12

THE RUSE

We had tried all evening to come up with a way to earn the ticket money. The next morning, when we met Dobbs in Covent Garden Market, our mission still looked impossible.

We sat on the stone steps of a church eating one-penny baked potatoes (Dobbs had bought them with his last pennies which he swore had not been stolen but given to him for carrying a lady's carpet bag) and trying to think of a way to earn a crown.

"Maybe we could borrow it from Inspector Janklow," I began, but I knew it was no good. Borrowing his money would mean involving him in our scheme. I bit my lip and tried to think of something else. "Or maybe we could sell something?"

Imogen's hands, still clutching her paper-wrapped potato, dropped to her lap. "Look at us, Katie. What have we got to sell? We're living off charity from a street urchin. No offence, Dobbs," she added.

Dobbs was busy alternating between stuffing his own

mouth with steaming potato and tossing chunks to Betsy who chomped and slobbered them up happily.

Imogen sighed a deflated sigh. "I hate feeling poor. What's the point of being rich if no one will take your money?"

"They'd take our money quick enough if they knew what it was," I said.

I watched Dobbs stuff the final third of the piping hot potato into his mouth.

"How do *you* make money, Dobbs? I mean, couldn't we do what you do and carry people's bags for them, or sweep streets or whatever it is you do?"

Dobbs looked a little embarrassed. "Don't take this personal, Miss Katie, but… well… you and Miss Imogen ain't really cut out for the Arab life. But don't let that discourage ya. To tell the truth, I don't deal much in money if I can 'elp it. I prefer the trade and barter system meself. Less counting of shillin's and pence and wot nots." He waved his hand as if he hadn't the time for such trivialities.

I perched my chin on top of my fists to think. "Well we can't very well barter our way into an art exhibition."

"I wouldn't be so sure," Dobbs said, standing up and brushing the crumbs from his breeches. "You just need a bit of ingenuity's all. What 'ave you got that's valuable to the likes of a Mr. Phineas Webb?"

I thought for a moment, then glanced at Imogen whose face was a complete blank. "I have no idea," she said flatly. "What could a famous artist possibly need…"

And suddenly, I thought of Tom Tippery, and a lightbulb clicked on in my head. "They need patrons! People to pay them money for their art. That's how they make a living."

"Ok." Imogen sounded unconvinced. "But, like we've just discussed, we don't *have* any money!"

"But your father does," I answered.

"My father?" She frowned. "How exactly is that supposed to help us?"

"Ok, look. I've got something... a way we wouldn't need money. In fact, we wouldn't actually have to *go* to the exhibition at all." The idea was playing itself out in my mind, but I wasn't quite sure Imogen would buy into it.

"Well go on then. Spit it out," she said testily.

"It would require a bit of acting..." I hesitated.

"Oh no." She glared. "Don't look at me like that, Katie."

"You only really need to be yourself, just pretending that your father is interested in buying some of Mr. Webb's paintings. Think about it. We could ambush Mr. Webb *after* the exhibition and try to get a private word with him away from the crowds."

She still looked dubious, but I knew all she needed was a bit more persuasion.

"Oh come on, Im," I pleaded. "We both know you're an amazing actress."

The corner of her mouth twitched, but she kept up the air of reluctance. "And what, may I ask, will *you* be doing in this charade?"

"I'll be your lady in waiting. I've had lots of practice playing that role with Sophia. The only problem is..." My mind went back to the lavish clothes the women at the Exhibition Room had worn. I looked down at my own rather plain blue chequered dress and then at Imogen's violet one. "We're going to need some nicer clothes if Phineas Webb is ever going to believe you're an aristocrat's daughter."

"Hmm," Imogen brushed the potato crumbs off her skirt. "Somehow I doubt we're going to find any furs or velvets in the charity cupboard at the Misses Turveys'."

"Need fine clothes, you say?" Dobbs had climbed up one of the church's columns and was peering out like a sailor from a crow's nest. He leapt down, straightened his coat and grinned a crooked, mischievous grin. "I can 'elp you there."

Dobbs said he'd be back in a flash. That was just before he climbed up an iron gate in the middle of a tall, brick wall, leapt into the snowy branches of a tree on the other side and disappeared. According to the clock on the church tower, he was back in under ten minutes. His smug face told us he'd been successful in his mission, whatever it was. The only clue to my eyes was that he returned a much fatter Dobbs than when he'd left.

"What happened to you?" Imogen eyed his bulging coat warily.

"Best I tell you in private. C'mon. Let's go to the Misses Turveys' an' I'll show you."

Once inside the hostel gates, Dobbs cast a wary look over both shoulders before unfastening his coat's two mismatched buttons. He pulled out a bundle of wadded up material which he unrolled to reveal two dresses.

"Hope these'll do. Didn't 'ave much time to consider me options." He held out a rich, velvety maroon dress for Imogen. "This one's a bit longer."

She took it and examined it with a slight look of surprise.

He then took the other bundle out from under his arm and unfurled a dark green silk dress with brass buttons. "For you, Miss Katie." Dobbs looked down at his feet and shuffled about in the snow. "Thought as it'd go nice with your ginger hair."

I felt my cheeks go hot and quickly cleared my throat. "I'm not taking that dress until you tell me where on earth you got it."

He raised his face sheepishly. "Wash line. See just over that wall? Tha's Henrietta Girls' School. There weren't a soul in the garden. Just lines and lines of fancy, frilly dresses and knickers."

"Dobbs, we can't wear *stolen* clothes!" I folded up the dress and held it out to him. "Take it back."

Imogen snickered.

"What's so funny?" I demanded.

Imogen cleared her throat and, without taking her eyes from the dress, muttered, "Just a bit rich coming from Katie Watson, the notorious horse thief."

I glared at her. "That was different."

Dobbs looked crestfallen. "Well I'm 'fraid I'm no good at sewing gowns, so either you'll 'aff to wear them dresses or give up the whole plan."

I couldn't argue with that point. Without the right clothing, my plan was a no-go. Reluctantly, I took the dress from him. "You're going back there and returning them the minute our mission is complete, got it?"

He shrugged. "If you like. Though I doubt them rich

girls would so much as notice one missing dress from the thousands."

A church bell tolled the half hour. Dobbs slapped his hand to his forehead. "Crikey, I 'bout forgot! I'm s'posed to meet the Inspector in 'alf an hour!" He spun around to make a dash for it, then spun back again. "Nearly forgot." Taking off his hat and flipping it upside down, he reached his arm in up to the elbow like a magician feeling for a white rabbit and pulled out two hats, one green and one maroon, two pairs of white gloves and two lace handkerchiefs.

Returning his own hat to its perch on his ears, he gave the rim a little tip and was off. We watched as he and Betsy leapt onto the back of an omnibus which carried them around the corner and away through the streets of London.

I was thinking how I should like to learn to catch a moving vehicle like that when Imogen sighed deeply.

"Well, what should we do first?" she asked, turning for the door. "Try on our new clothes or do our homework?"

That was easy. "I'm dying to find out what's in that folder," I answered. By the time we'd got back to the privacy of our room the night before, it had been too dark to properly sort through the contents of the Phineas Webb files, and I had been itching to discover what information the Inspector had collected on him. "We've only got a few hours before the exhibition opens. I want to get through as much of it as we can so we know who we're dealing with."

An hour later, I sat sprawled over documents on the bed while Imogen twisted around with the tiny hand mirror trying to see the back of her dress. "That Dobbs might have a future career in fashion. This fits like it was made for me, don't you think?"

"What?" I glanced up for half a second – "Oh, yea. Looks lovely." – and resumed reading the newspaper clipping I was in the middle of. It was a review by an art critic from many years earlier. "Listen to this, Im." I cleared my throat and read:

Since his earliest days in the Royal Academy, Mr. Webb has stood apart from his peers as a daring artist with little regard for the rules of classical painting. He has controversially been known to portray the scenes from the Scriptures and even the Holy Family with shocking naturalism, causing the viewer to blush as if he were peering through a vestry window at these sacred events.

But never before has Mr. Webb's naturalism risen to such a height as in his newest and most lauded work, The Wedding Feast. *The eternal banquet itself brings to mind a heraldic scene, perhaps a feast at the mythic King Arthur's table. The painting is executed with such a sense of reality, such an attention to detail, that it is almost impossible to believe Mr. Webb did not, by some magic, journey to medieval times himself, the way the naturalist travels to the Galapagos Islands to bring back living specimens. Webb's paintings admittedly do not have a heartbeat, but they are all but alive.*

"Katie, you really ought to get dressed. We'll be late."

I pulled my eyes away from the review. But as I undressed, the line kept playing itself over in my head. *"By some magic..."* Could there really be some magic in Phineas Webb's painting, or was this just the critic's imaginative style? I felt the old tingling sensation. Could it mean that, perhaps, we were getting closer to Ramona?

My mind was full of possibilities as I pulled on the green dress. "We can't botch this up tonight," I said as Imogen fastened up the back.

"You're the one who wanted *me* to do the acting, you know."

"I know," I admitted. "And you'll do a great job. I just meant ... I feel like we're on to something here. I don't want to blow it when we might be getting close."

Imogen walked around to face me and braced my shoulders. "Just try to calm down Katie. We just got here a couple days ago, remember? You know I want to find Ramona too, but just don't get your hopes up *too* high."

I nodded, but inside, my heart was galloping with expectation. Phineas Webb just *had* to be the key to unlock this mystery.

THE BELLS TOLLED seven o'clock just as we took cover in the shadows of the triple-arched carriageway of Somerset House.

"What am I supposed to do with this handkerchief?" Imogen stuffed the cloth into her neckline, shook her head and pulled it out again.

"I don't know. Just carry it, I suppose." I reached up to make sure my little straw brimmed hat was straight, then took a bracing breath. "Ready?"

"Yup." Imogen nodded, then, "Oh wait." She stuffed the handkerchief up one of her ruffled sleeves. "Ok."

We linked arms the way we'd seen so many elegant

ladies do, and stepped out into a pool of gaslight. There were crowds of people locked in enthusiastic conversation coming out of the open doors of the Exhibition Rooms. Two policemen stood on either side of the door. One of them caught my eye, and I quickly turned away, taking Imogen with me.

"How are we supposed to have a private word with Phineas Webb if all these people are waiting to see him?" Imogen whispered.

I shook my head, frustrated with myself. Why hadn't I bargained on all of Mr. Webb's admirers having the same bright idea to ambush him outside of the Exhibition Room? Only now did I realise how outlandish my idea had been, like trying to get an autograph from a Victorian rock star.

The sound of hooves drew my eye to the carriageway where a pair of beautiful white horses pulled a luxurious carriage. The driver, a man in a tall top hat, called them to a halt in the middle of the carriageway and looked at a small door in the passage as if waiting for someone to come through it.

I gasped. "Come with me," I whispered, taking Imogen's arm.

"Where are we going?"

"Remember what Janklow said about Phineas Webb? How he's a hermit and avoids crowds?"

A light switched on in Imogen's eyes. "You think that could be his getaway carriage?"

Just then, the side door opened, and two men stepped briskly out. The first wore a turban. He opened the carriage door and took out a fur blanket from inside. The other man was casting about anxiously, as if hoping not to be seen. He was very tall and impressive, even in the dim lighting, with thick, bushy sideburns that came right down to his chin.

Although the picture I had seen of Phineas Webb in the case file was from his younger days, there was no mistaking the dignified face. "That's him," I said hoarsely in Imogen's ear, and gave her arm a tug. "Quick, before he gets into the carriage!"

Without a second's hesitation, she rushed forward waving her hand as if to flag him down. "Oh, Mr. Webb. Thank heavens we haven't missed you!"

He froze, his foot was already on the step. Then, cautiously, he peered around the carriage door.

Imogen, like a champion, dove right into conversation as if the whole thing had been rehearsed. "Oh, Mr. Webb, we've had such bad luck, you've no idea. I'm so glad we caught you. My father is the *greatest* admirer of your work. He wanted to attend the exhibition more than *anything* but he couldn't because... because he's away on business in..."

I caught up to her just in time to blurt out, "India!"

"Exactly," Imogen said with a nod. "He's in India working for... the Queen. So he sent me on his behalf. I'm very interested in art, you see. And–"

"Pardon me, Miss." Mr. Webb interrupted. He shook his head as if clearing it. "Your Father is...?"

"Oh, how silly of me not to say. Lord Humphreys. You've probably heard of him?" Imogen paused hopefully.

My heart pumped audibly.

"Or if you've not heard of him, I'm sure that's because

he spends such a lot of his time in India... on business for the Queen."

Mr. Webb seemed to be searching his memory. "Yes. Yes, I dare say. Lord Humphreys. The name does ring a bell. And do I understand that your father has sent you to advise him on the purchase of one of my new paintings?"

"Exactly. Only, unfortunately," Imogen became suddenly forlorn, "our horse went lame on the way here and we've missed the exhibition. Such a pity... but maybe next time..." We both curtseyed and slowly, as slowly as we could manage, began to turn away. My heart was in my throat.

"Wait."

My heart skipped a beat. We turned back to find Mr. Webb fingering for something inside his coat.

"Why don't you come for a private viewing of the paintings at my home. Would tomorrow at noon suit you? I shall have my butler set out a light luncheon." He offered Imogen the card. In the carriage's lamp light, its gold letters glimmered.

Imogen took it. "Awesome!" She froze as soon as the word left her mouth.

I glanced sideways at Imogen who looked petrified at Mr. Webb.

He looked confused. "I beg your pardon?"

"I meant," Imogen cleared her throat, "I can hardly wait to see your *AWE*-inspiring work, Mr. Webb. Thank you for this wonderful opportunity."

He bowed. "Bid you good evening." We watched the painter climb into his carriage, and the servant cover his lap with the fur blanket. The driver cracked his whip, the white horses sprang into an elegant trot, turning about in the courtyard past all the waiting admirers and out again through the carriageway.

Only when the carriage was out of sight did Imogen and I do something that I confess was *not* very detective-like. We clasped hands and jumped up and down.

"We did it!" she shrieked.

"*You* did it!" I said, laughing. "That was your best performance yet!"

"Except for that one little slip." She covered her eyes with her hands. "Awesome?"

"But you recovered brilliantly," I reassured her.

"You think?" She smiled. "Guess I was rather good, wasn't I?" She tucked the little card with the gold inscription *Phineas Warwick Webb* into her jacket pocket, then linked her arm through mine. "You know, when we get back home, I might just try out for the school play."

13

THE LADY OF CAMELOT

We spent the next morning in our room getting ready for our private visit with Phineas Webb. I pored feverishly over the art reviews and newspaper clippings in the folder while Imogen practiced putting on aristocratic airs.

"If only I'd known, I would have watched a few more costume dramas before coming here," she lamented.

"Oh, you'll do fine. Although…"

"Although what?" she demanded.

I smiled. "It might not be a bad idea to practice your Queens' English… you know, just to avoid any more slips like yesterday's."

She crossed her arms defensively over her chest. "I speak Queen's English. I *am* English, remember?"

I kept my eyes firmly on the article I'd been reading. "Yes, but you speak a different Queen's English to Phineas Webb. Maybe if you read a few of these articles, it'll help you make the switch from Elizabeth II to Victoria."

She sank onto the bed with a frustrated sigh and began

rifling through the stacks of papers I'd so carefully sorted into reviews, articles, letters and photographs, and then again by date.

"On second thought,"– I winced – "why don't I just read out to you the notes I've made so far. The most important thing is that you appear to know something about Phineas Webb's paintings."

She stopped rifling and fell back onto the bed. "Go on, then. Brief me on the facts, Watson."

"Okay." I cleared my throat. "First of all, the reviews show a sort of pattern. In Webb's early days at the Academy, people couldn't get enough of him. Even Charles Dickens and the famous critic John Ruskin thought he was the best thing since Michelangelo. It seems his paintings were unlike anything people had ever seen. And he had a sort of brotherhood of other young artists that wanted to paint like he did. They believed that the best art was medieval art, and that England ought to return to a sort of heraldic age."

"You mean like Webb's exhibition? The Age of Chivalry? King Arthur and Queen Guinevere, and Lancelot and all that?"

I nodded. "They even called themselves the Round Table, only Webb was definitely their Arthur by the looks of it. Even his younger brother had to live in his shadow."

"Ouch. So his brother was a painter too?"

I nodded. "There's a photo of them together in here somewhere, when they were young." I flipped through the stack of images until I found what I was looking for.

Imogen sat up and looked over my shoulder at the photograph. It was a little faded, but someone had handwritten beneath it, *Gabriel and Phineas Webb, Royal Academy Annual Exhibition, 1848*. Taken over thirty-five years ago. The two handsome, distinguished young men stood with their arms around one another's shoulders.

"Huh. Well that's interesting." Imogen fell back again. "What's next?"

I slipped the photograph into the flap in the back cover of my detective notebook – I'd examine it more closely later – then flipped back to my notes. "Right. There are a bunch of articles about *The Wedding Feast*. You know, the stolen painting," I added, seeing Imogen's confused look. "It went on a world tour, and it seems everyone who was anyone saw it: maharajas, the Emperor of Russia, even the Pope."

Imogen pulled a face. "What's so special about it?"

I shook my head. "I guess it was just ... different. But after that painting, he kind of lost his touch."

"What do you mean?"

"Well, apparently, after 1851, nobody liked a single painting he did. There's not a single good review. They're all brutal. The newspaper articles say Phineas Webb had to sell *The Wedding Feast* to St. Paul's Cathedral just to keep from going bankrupt."

Imogen scratched her head. "So ... explain how he's now the best thing to come to England since Victoria sponge cake?"

"Because of this." I handed her a bundle of articles and pointed to the titles: *Phineas Warwick Webb re-emerges like a phoenix from the ashes. The Muses revisit Phineas Warwick Webb. Phineas Warwick Webb to be knighted on New Year's Eve in honour of his contribution to Great Britain's artistic milieu.*

"Strange, isn't it?" Imogen said through a yawn.

"Think you can remember all this when you meet him?" I asked, trying not to sound worried.

"Sure I can." Then noting my less-than-confident expression, she added, "Well he's not exactly going to give me a quiz on his life, is he?"

"Don't forget what Inspector Janklow said. No direct or overly personal questions. We've got one chance, so we can't afford to put him off. Stick to flattery and keep him talking as much as possible."

"I've got it, I've got it." She lazily moved to the window and gazed out, then twirled around. "Oh crumbs! It's half past eleven! We've got to get all the way to Bloomsbury in half an hour, *and* it looks like it's going to rain."

My heart skipped a beat. How had we forgotten the time? "We really need to get a watch," I said, stuffing my detective notebook into my bag. We both grabbed our hats and bolted out the door and down the first flight of steps, nearly colliding with Agatha Turvey who was just emerging from her bedroom.

"Good heavens!" she cried, leaning against the wall with one hand to her forehead.

We both apologised, though she hardly seemed to hear us.

With a whimper she said, "I've been meaning to ask… about your father… the donation…"

"Oh yes," Imogen said. "He wrote this morning about it, Miss Turvey."

Before she could ask any more questions, we flew

down the next flight of stairs with Miss Turvey's moans of "Oh, my poor nerves" following us out the door.

We were in such a hurry, we didn't even notice the bulldog or the jutting-out ears of the figure leaning against the gate.

"Oi! Wha's the rush?"

"Dobbs?" Now I was looking right at him, but I hardly believed my eyes that this was the same boy. He had the same impish face sure enough, though several shades cleaner. He had on a new pair of fitting trousers, polished leather boots with no holes, and a tidy, brown jacket with all its buttons intact. When he removed his wool cap, I was shocked to see a valiant attempt had been made to comb his lion-like hair down flat.

"You look… different," I said, unable to hide my surprise. I looked down and noticed even Betsy's coat gleamed with cleanliness.

Ears glowing, he rubbed his nose on his clean sleeve. "Inspector Janklow said I 'ad to look respectable if I was to pass as your chaperone. Mrs. Janklow stitched these up for me." He tugged at his trouser leg. "Feels a bit like spreadin' butter on bacon, if you ask me. But Janklow's the boss, so…"

An awkward moment passed in which we all just stood looking at each other before Dobbs remembered something and snapped his fingers. "I was to deliver a message. Janklow says meet him at the tea shop outside St. Paul's at three o'clock, if that suits you. An' Mrs. Janklow says come 'round for a cup o' tea whenever you like in the meantime."

"What happened to all your suspicion that Inspector

Janklow is in cahoots with the bobbies?" Imogen asked snidely.

"On me honour," Dobbs said, solemnly laying his hand over his heart, "Inspector Janklow 'n' his missus are the finest folk in her Majesty's Kingdom. Gave Bess 'n' me the first bed as we can remember sleeping in … though Mrs. Janklow did make us both wash 'afore she'd let us into it."

Imogen sniffed the air in Dobbs's direction. "So she did. Not bad, Dobbs."

"You two don't look 'alf shabby yourselves," Dobbs commented with a nod to our new clothes.

"We'll look shabby soon enough in this mizzle," Imogen groaned.

Sure enough, beads of mist clung to the strands of hair around her face. Soon our borrowed fine clothes would look just like bags of soggy fabric.

"Dobbs, we've got to get to Bloomsbury, and quick," I explained. "We're having tea with Phineas Webb in twenty minutes. Know any short cuts?"

His mouth and eyes had grown circular. "Tea with Phineas… God 'elp you, you'll be a right mess if you walk up to Bloomsbury in this stuff. He'll never take you for ladies then. 'Ow 'bout I call you a cab?"

"We still haven't got any money, remember?" Imogen said impatiently.

Dobbs reached into his pocket and pulled out a handful of coins.

I gave him a look. "Where did that come from?"

"It's clean money, I swear it! The Inspector said I was to earn respectf'ly. Made me spend the whole afternoon blacking shoes outside the Temple Courts." He showed us both his hands which were covered in black shoe polish.

I smiled my approval. "Feels good doing honest work, doesn't it?"

He looked uncertainly at a big blister on his thumb and grimaced. "Not sure I'd go as far as that."

Dobbs managed to flag down a cab in ten seconds flat, much to the relief of the swarming butterflies in my stomach. At least we were going to get there on time. As to what happened *when* we got there... We would cross that bridge soon enough. Or sink in the attempt.

"Wha's the address?" The cabbie grunted.

Imogen read it off the card: "Number sixty-four, Bloomsbury Square Gardens."

The cabbie sat up straight, then turned on his perch and gave us a look as if he'd just seen a ghost. "I know the place. Phineas Warwick Webb's house. Took a young lady there once before. Beautiful lady she was."

My tummy butterflies took off swarming again, and the words tumbled out of my mouth. "Was she dark? With dark hair?"

He gawked. "Tha's right. Sorta exotic like, she was. But 'ow'd you–"

"How long ago?" I interrupted. My heart was in my mouth.

He bit his thumbnail in thought for what felt like a long moment. "Law, must've been 'bout this time last year. Tha's right. Was 'bout the new year."

Imogen and I looked at each other. "Thank you," I said to the cabbie, and we leapt into his cab as fast as our petticoats would allow.

It was raining hard when we drove up along a row of beautiful brick houses lining the four sides of a snow-covered garden square. All the houses looked the same, except for the colour of their doors... all except the last one on the row. It was twice as big, half-hidden by hedges and creeping vines, and enclosed by a tall iron gate. A brown-skinned man with a turban stood at the gate with a crimson umbrella. I thought it was the strangest sight, and then I realised the cab was stopping in front of the house. The man in the turban approached the cab as if he'd been expecting our arrival and opened the door.

"Miss Humphreys, I believe?" he said in an air of perfect gentility, then held out his hand and helped Imogen, then me out of the cab, all the while holding his crimson umbrella over our heads with the other hand.

We paid the cabbie, then followed the man up the stone path to the house's entrance beneath a grand, pointed archway. Dobbs and Betsy followed behind, getting drenched.

After he had led us into the foyer, the man in the turban turned and looked down his long, straight nose at Dobbs. "Perhaps the gentleman and his dog would like to dry themselves by the kitchen fire? I will show you. And may I take the ladies' shawls and bags?"

I thanked him and handed over my shawl.

"And madam's bag?"

I handed over my satchel somewhat reluctantly; but it wasn't as if I'd be able to take notes while we were right under Phineas Webb's nose, so I let it go. He bowed, then addressed Dobbs. "Right this way, if you please."

As the two of them turned down a corridor to the left, a

maid entered the foyer. She greeted us politely with an efficient curtsey, but not warmly. "Mr. Webb welcomes you to Camelot." Again she curtseyed, then offered us each a beautifully embroidered cashmere shawl.

Catching each other's wowed eyes, we wrapped the shawls around our shoulders and followed the maid into the main entrance. If I'd been wowed before, I was floored now. In front of us was a carved wooden staircase with golden banisters. Lanterns with coloured glass hung from chains attached to a ceiling so high up above, it could not be seen. The walls were wild with prints of peacocks, hares, dogs and vines, and a great black bear rug carpeted the floor at the foot of the stair.

"Mr. Webb requests that you wait for him in the gallery," the maid said, shaking us out of our amazed stupor. We followed her down a long corridor with violet silk-covered walls and golden vaulted ceilings. We passed marble statues of saints and fauns, suits of armour and heraldic shields, and finally stopped at a carved wooden door beneath a pointed arch. Two gargoyle heads stared at us from either side of the door as the maid opened it and invited us to pass through.

It became instantly clear why the two gargoyles were stationed outside the door. They were guarding a treasure vault. The room we entered was the most stunning part of the house yet: a large, hexagonal room lit by stained glass windows and a single skylight high above in the vaulted ceiling. The walls were canary yellow and adorned with tapestries of medieval banquets. There was a tea table in front of a giant stone hearth surrounded by expensive-looking, cushiony furniture.

Perhaps most extraordinary of all were the bird cages. At least a dozen of them hung near the stained glass windows inhabited by the most exotic-looking birds, each chirping and whistling its own unique song. They were so beautiful, and yet I felt sad to hear them calling and cooing from behind bars. *They should be free,* I thought. *Not used for decoration.*

"This place is insane," Imogen whispered as the maid pulled the door closed and left us alone. "It's like Cinderella's castle meets the Hunchback of Notre Dame. No wonder Phineas Webb hardly ever leaves home."

I slowly revolved on the spot, taking in the fairy world we had stumbled upon, then stopped. There was so much to see in the room, I hadn't noticed a row of easels lined up on the far side, each one with a covered canvas. "Do you think those are the paintings we've come to look at?" I asked, checking the door over my shoulder as I moved for a closer look.

Imogen followed on my heels. "Only one way to find out."

I reached out and caught the corner of one of the velvet covers. Carefully peeling it back, I caught my breath and heard Imogen's breath catch beside me.

The painting was beyond beautiful, all in deep, rich, earthy colours. It showed a window in a stone tower surrounded by a moat. Wisteria vines grew up the tower and framed the window, drawing my eye to look inside. When I did, my eyes met the dark, glistening eyes of a woman with long, flowing black hair. She appeared as proud and lovely as a Queen, yet as lonely as a lost child. She was as exotic and wild as Webb's birds and, like them, had a sad longing for freedom in her eyes. I knew her at once, and my heart reached out to her with an aching longing to unlock her tower door and set her free. She was, after all, my great-great-great-grandmother.

"Ah, I see you've met my lady," a deep, velvety voice spoke from behind. My hand dropped, letting the cover fall.

14

CLOCKWORK CANARY

"Miss Humphreys." Phineas Webb took Imogen's hand in his and held it to his lips, revealing his full head of thick grey hair. He looked older than I had thought last night.

"And I don't believe I've had the pleasure of learning your friend's name."

"Oh, sorry." Imogen presented me. "This is my cousin, Katie Watson. She's a great admirer of your paintings as well, Mr. Webb."

"Enchanted." I observed him as he bent over to kiss my hand as well. He was still very handsome for a man rather older than my dad, and was dressed to the hilt in a peacock-blue waistcoat and paisley cravat. But his eyes had the far-off look of someone who is weary with the world. There was something familiar in that look too, though I couldn't think why.

He turned to the paintings and lifted the velvet curtain I had let drop, then proceeded to lift the other covers from the other canvases, all but one. As my eyes flitted from one painting to the next, my heart all the while raced faster. Every single painting featured a woman I knew could only be Ramona, each time depicted as a medieval maiden, and each time with the same sad eyes.

Mr. Webb cleared his throat, making me suddenly aware that he was waiting for our reaction.

"They're wonderful," I said enthusiastically.

"Yes, the reviews were right, Mr. Webb," Imogen chimed in enthusiastically. "I do feel transported to an age of chivalry just looking at these. My Father will just adore them."

The smallest, polite smile appeared on his lips. "I am pleased to hear your father favours the bygone days as I do. There are very few modern men who appreciate the greatness of our lost past." He paused a moment, transfixed on the painting of the woman in the tower, then seemed to come back to himself. "All of these you see represent women of the Arthurian Legends. Here, as you can see, I've depicted the Lady of Shalott." He moved on to the next canvas. "And here we have Nymue, the Lady of the Lake, offering Arthur the sword Excalibur."

"And what's under here?" In Imogen's show of enthusiasm, she had rushed past Phineas to lift the cover of the final painting.

"That is—" Phineas held up his hand to stop her, but too late. The cover dropped to the floor revealing an only partially painted canvas, the beginning outlines of a king and queen sitting on thrones. "Unfinished." Hastily, he swept up the velvet cover from the floor and threw it back over the canvas. He didn't turn back to us immediately, but seemed to be gathering himself. When at last he did turn, there was the same polite smile, still in place. "Excuse me," he said apologetically. "It is just that I never reveal my works in progress. I find it spoils the final effect."

Imogen's cheeks glowed. She seemed to have lost confidence and gave me a pleading look for help.

"I... I was wondering, Mr. Webb," I launched in without knowing where I was going, "about the lady in your paintings. I've never seen anyone quite like her. Is she someone you know?"

I watched him closely, but his face didn't betray the least sign of emotion. After a moment in which he toyed with a ring on his little finger, he answered matter-of-factly, "She was my housekeeper, years ago. An exceptional beauty. She possessed such a... an otherworldly aura, I was simply compelled to paint her."

"Your housekeeper?" I repeated, trying to sound much less interested than I really was. In reality, the next question was ready to explode from my lips; but I took a breath and smiled. "And ... you said she *was* your housekeeper. Does she still work for you? I mean," – I cast a glance at the paintings – "you *still* paint her, don't you?"

The searching look he gave me, as if he'd just seen me for the first time, caught me off-guard. "From memory, yes," he answered.

My heart plummeted into my stomach. "Memory?"

"But," he continued, "my memories of her are as vibrant as if they were made only yesterday."

"But you don't mean..." I was afraid to ask, but I had to. "She didn't..."

"She never belonged to this city," he cut me off. "Or

this world of machines and soot and modern madness. No." His eyes swept lovingly over *The Lady of Shalott*. "She belonged to *that* world. A world of beauty, chivalry, fantasies come true."

I felt my legs giving out beneath me for fear of what this meant. It was too straightforward a question, but I had to know the truth. "Mr. Webb, you're not saying she's dead?"

To my bewilderment, he actually smiled, as if the idea amused him. "Dead, Miss Watson? How could she be dead? I have made her immortal."

I cast a confused look at Imogen where she stood just behind Phineas.

He caught the look and chuckled. "In my paintings, of course. In my paintings."

Then, with such a sudden shift in mood that it left my head spinning, he said cheerfully, "But how very bullish of me not to offer you any refreshment! I did ask my butler for tea on the quarter of the hour precisely."

He reached into his waistcoat pocket and brought out the most extraordinary pocketwatch. When he gave it a flip with his thumb, a tiny golden canary bird popped up and began actually to flap its delicate golden wings and chirp.

It had only sung the first few notes of a melody when a tingle travelled up my spine. I could tell from Imogen's eyes, as round as Miss Turvey's currant buns, that she recognised the song too. It was the very same sad, sweet song Ka-Ti had sung to bring the painted horses to life. Ramona's song.

Mr. Webb snapped the pocketwatch shut with an

abruptness that shattered the song's spell but left me in a daze.

"What an extraordinary watch," Imogen was saying. "Wherever did you get it? I must ask my father for one just like it."

"I found it. At a pawn shop," Mr. Webb answered disinterestedly. "I thought it pretty, and as you can see, I have a fascination with birds. I carry this little canary in my pocket as a sort of good luck charm."

"Oh, may I see?" Imogen held out her gloved hand with an innocent, girlish expression.

Mr. Webb eyed her hand for a moment, then smiled and placed the watch in it. "Of course."

"Look, Katie." Imogen held up the watch so that I could get a better look at it. "Isn't it sweet?"

"Mmhmm," I answered, perusing the watch for a clue, perhaps an engraving of a name. I found only the tiny inscription *Salomon & Botts* etched into the back case with a crack down the middle. The case appeared to have been broken in two, then welded back together.

"Ah, here is the tea now," Mr. Webb said brightly as the door opened and a trio of maids entered with silver trays. He held out his hand for the pocketwatch, then returned it to his waistcoat pocket before offering us each an arm and leading us to the cushiony sofas.

An extravagant spread of sandwiches, scones and cakes was laid before us, but my mind was far too agitated to leave room for an appetite. I filled my plate, though, while trying desperately to think of some way of bringing up the subject of Mr. Webb's model again. But it was no good. Mr. Webb was asking questions of his own about

Imogen's father and his work in India. Something he was saying caught my attention.

"I quite understand the challenges of living in two different worlds at once." He paused to take a gentlemanly sip from his teacup, then continued. "My work often takes me abroad. In fact, I only just arrived back to London in time for the exhibition yesterday."

"Oh? Where did you go?" Imogen asked in her girlish way that was so disarming. "Somewhere exciting?"

Mr. Webb appeared to be lost in his teacup as he gave the answer. "Somewhere very, very far from here." He took another sip.

"And what are you planning on painting next?" Imogen asked when he'd risen out of his cup and placed it on the tea table.

He sat back and crossed his legs. "As a matter of fact, I am approaching the end of my career. You may have heard, but I am to be knighted by Her Majesty on New Year's Eve at Buckingham Palace. That night shall also mark my retirement."

"You mean you aren't going to paint anymore?" Imogen asked in a tone of concern.

Phineas thought a moment before answering. "I may. But I should like to try some new venture. Leave London and all of its raucous and ugly machinery."

His words struck panic in me. He meant to leave London in only a few days' time, which meant our chances of finding out what he knew of Ramona were quickly running out. In a moment of recklessness, I asked, "Will you see your housekeeper before you go?"

"My housekeeper?" His look was uncertain.

"I mean the one from the paintings. Your model. She lives in London, doesn't she?"

As soon as I'd asked it, I knew I'd gone too far. His whole body went stiff, his expression cold and distant. As if he hadn't heard me at all, he stood. "Thank you for favouring me, ladies. If you'll excuse me, I have some pressing matters." He bowed and left the room before we could so much as stand to curtsey.

15

DISAPPOINTMENT AND DEDUCTIONS

"Well? 'Ow'd it go?" Dobbs asked in a confidential whisper as soon as we were on the other side of Camelot's iron gates.

"*Imogen* was brilliant," I grumbled, causing Dobbs to take a step away from me as we crossed the street to Bloomsbury Square Gardens. I could have kicked myself if I hadn't been wearing a skirt and petticoat. "How could I be so stupid?" I groaned, running my hands down my face in utter self-contempt.

"You weren't stupid, Katie." Imogen rested her arm over my shoulder. "How could you have known he would react like that?"

I made straight for a bench under a knobbly old chestnut tree and sank down onto it, regretting it a moment later when dampness soaked through my skirt. "I can't believe after telling *you* to be careful, I'm the one who went and scared him off. I completely blew it."

Imogen slumped down on the wet bench beside me. Meanwhile, Dobbs propped himself against the tree and

Betsy rooted for chestnuts in the wet dirt. "I really think you're being too hard on yourself," she said. "And anyway, you didn't blow it. The very fact that he responded the way he did means something."

I lifted my face out of my hands and looked her in the eye. "That's what I thought too. But Im, what if it means something... something bad?" I couldn't bring myself to say what I feared. "He looked sort of... hurt, didn't he? And all that about immortalising her... about her not belonging to this world... Im, what if Ramona is... you don't think she's..."

"If she were dead, he would've just said so," she answered confidently. "Sounds more to me like she ran off and broke his heart."

I looked at her surprised. "You think so?"

She rolled her eyes. "Honestly, Katie. You're a great detective, but you don't know the first thing about romance. Why would he paint all those pictures of Ramona as Guinevere and himself as Arthur if he wasn't in love with her?"

"So you thought Arthur looked like Webb too?"

"It was obvious. Embarrassing, really."

My mouth dropped open, self-hatred giving way to excitement. "And what about the musical pocketwatch? I nearly choked when I heard the song come out of that little canary."

Imogen nodded enthusiastically. "I bet that's why he lied about where he got it. It must have been a gift from her. He finds it too painful to remember!"

If Imogen was right, Phineas Webb's coldness and hermit tendencies made sense. I felt sorry for him, alone with a broken heart all those years. But my sympathy didn't rub out the frustration of *not* knowing where Ramona had gone. Something was missing from the whole picture.

I shut my eyes and rubbed my temples, trying with all my brainpower to find it. "How can we be so close, but still feel so far from finding her?" I muttered. "If we only knew who stole Webb's painting... who put the magic one in its place... That has to be the missing piece, surely."

A strange gurgling sound from the oak tree caused Imogen and me to turn. Dobbs's ears were glowing again, and he was hugging his middle. "Wot?" he said defensively. "*Some* of us wasn't offered anyfink to eat with our tea."

"Oh, sorry Dobbs." I opened the flap of my bag, dug in and pulled out the bun wrapped in my handkerchief. "Here, I've got a bun saved from breakfast in my bag."

Dobbs took it gratefully and threw Betsy a chunk before cramming the rest into his own mouth. My hand, meanwhile, hovered over my open bag. Something felt off.

"Hang on a minute." I pried open the bag and peered inside, then reached my hand in again and felt all the way around the inner lining. In a flash of horror, I realised what was missing. "My detective notebook. It's gone."

"What?" Now Imogen grabbed the bag off my lap and tried her luck. "But that doesn't make sense. I saw you put it in there before we left the hostel. And who would take your notebook?"

Without meaning to, both of our heads turned towards Dobbs whose cheeks were swollen to bursting with bun.

"Wot you lookin' at me for?" he protested, sending bits

of bun bursting from his stuffed cheeks. He gulped down his mouthful. "Ain't that nice. Soon as somefink goes missin', ol' Dobbs must be the culprit. Well, you can search me." He held up his hands. "These 'ands is clean."

"Get a grip. We're not blaming you," Imogen snapped, though I'm sure she felt as ashamed as I did for suspecting him.

"I'll bet it was that manservant chap with the towel wrapped about 'is 'ead," Dobbs said confidentially.

Imogen shot him one of her withering glares. "It wasn't a towel, it was a turban. And that's a ridiculous idea. What would a famous painter's manservant want with Katie's notebook? Only a pickpocket would think to suspect him."

"Reckon it takes one to know one," Dobbs muttered hotly.

Imogen rolled her eyes.

I stayed out of the argument and focused on mentally retracing my steps. "It was definitely here when we arrived in the cab," I said. "I'm absolutely sure of that."

"Don't guess you might have left it in the cab?" Imogen suggested.

I shook my head. "I never took it out of the bag."

"Maybe it fell out. Look, don't worry. If you try, I bet you can remember most of what you'd written and just copy it down again."

I closed my eyes, mentally flipping through the pages and pages of notes I'd scribbled. "It was mostly a bunch of notes from the Phineas Webb file... and the photograph of him and his brother... oh yeah,"– I winced as I remembered– "and Inspector Janklow's card... *and* the Misses

Turveys' address, so that if the notebook did go missing someone might find it and know where to return it."

"Oh, well, nothing to worry about, then," Imogen said with false chirpiness. "Whoever finds it will only know where we're staying and who we're working for. No big deal!"

My head found its way once again into my hands. "This has not been a good day for me."

"Cheer up, Miss Katie," I felt Dobbs's hand rest on my shoulder. "It may be that Inspector Janklow's got some news that'll brighten you up. Or at least he might 'ave an idea as to how to find a missing notebook being a detective 'n' all."

I nodded but said nothing. Imogen got up to go. I let her and Dobbs walk on a few paces; then, feeling I'd rather just sit there in soggy misery, I pulled myself up and muttered under my breath, "I'm supposed to be one too."

WE TOOK an omnibus to Charing Cross and walked along the Thames path to St. Paul's Cathedral to avoid the crowded Strand. Inspector Janklow was waiting for us at the bottom of the cathedral steps. A pipe was clenched between his teeth, and he was just consulting his pocketwatch as we walked up.

"Ah, just in time," he said. "I've an errand for you, Arthur." I realised he was speaking to Dobbs as the boy came to attention. "You'll find a certain diminutive man by the name of Mortimer working at the John Soane Museum in Lincoln's Inn Fields. Ask for him and tell him I will meet him at the Seven Stars within half the hour. I owe him a drink."

"A' once, sir." Dobbs tipped the brim of his new woollen cap, turned on his heels like a soldier, and he and Betsy scampered away on their errand.

Janklow watched him go, thoughtfully smoking his pipe, then turned to Imogen and me. "And did you ladies meet with any success on your little off-the-books mission?" He tapped his finger to his nose as he said *off-the-books*.

"Oh, just a little," Imogen said, hardly containing her self-satisfaction. "We've just had tea with Phineas Webb *and* a private viewing of his paintings at his home."

Inspector Janklow lowered the pipe and gave us both a long, hard look. "And what in heaven's name did you say to charm him so? I do hope no laws were broken in the process?"

"Not unless flattery and little white lies are against the law," Imogen said innocently. "All part of the detective's toolbox, right?"

I thought the Inspector looked rather uncomfortable. "As are dignity and self-restraint."

"Don't worry," I assured him. "We just showed a little more interest in patronising his paintings than we could actually afford. No harm was done."

Janklow raised his eyebrows. "Ingenious, I must say. But, Miss Watson, if you don't mind my mentioning, you do look a little out of sorts. Was Mr. Webb not the lead to your missing relation that you'd hoped for?"

"Not exactly, but–" I told him about the Camelot paintings and how Webb had been reluctant to say much at all about Ramona. Imogen added her theory of Webb's having been thwarted in love.

Inspector Janklow listened intently, the ridges on his forehead kneading in thought all the while. "There may be something in all of this. The man is a walking mystery, make no mistake. And speaking of mysteries, shall we inspect the scene of the crime together?"

A man in a long, white robe met us at the door of the cathedral and led us down to the crypt where hung the painting I knew so well by now. An area around the painting had been roped off, but Janklow lifted the rope and invited us to join him inside.

"What we have here, ladies, is a classic 'locked room' scenario," he began. "The cleric assures me that all external doors were locked. He personally bolted the western doors and side exits. He has vouched that *The Wedding Feast* was there one moment, then gone the very next. The police were sent for immediately, and, as you know, two young ladies were seen moments later running from the western portal."

Imogen flew to our defence. "That's because we were locked in. We didn't–"

Janklow held up his hands. "This is not an interrogation, Miss Humphreys. Reason supports that even two such capable and independent young ladies could not carry away a painting of that magnitude. I am merely stating *all* the facts of the case."

Imogen squirmed at my side, but said nothing.

Janklow began to pace back and forth as he continued. "Now, the theft may appear to be the work of a ghost or spirit, but of course the one thing we can be certain of is a rational explanation. You have already dispelled one impossibility by telling me that in fact the cathedral was not empty on the night of the theft. The two of you were inside. And who is to say someone else was not, unbeknown to you both, lurking in the shadows? At least we can be certain we are dealing with flesh and blood."

Imogen and I shot a quick glance at one another.

"Look closely, Miss Watson. Do you detect any other signs or clues that might shed light on the crime?" Janklow stood back, giving me an invitation to get closer to the painting.

I took a deep breath to focus. Nervously, I stepped up, trying to think back to all the Sherlock Holmes stories I had read. Imagining what Sherlock would do on the scene of a crime, I raked over the painting with my eyes, left to right, top to bottom. With every sweep of my eyes, my heart raced a little faster. I half expected the painting to come alive at any moment. I hoped it would; then Janklow would see for himself. But it remained still and lifeless like any ordinary painting.

When my eyes reached the bottom of the frame, I squinted to make out a tiny object in the right-hand corner. "There's something here. A little sketch. A bird, perhaps?" A bird. Ramona drew a kingfisher on all of her sketches. Could it be? "It could be some sort of signature," I suggested.

Janklow took a monocle from his breast pocket and leaned in for a look. "I confess I hadn't noticed it before. Very good, Miss Watson. You might be on to something there. Anything else?"

My eyes moved outside the painting, wandering about

the wall. "There," I said, pointing to a mark in the plaster just above the picture frame. "Looks like the thief was in a hurry to hang the painting and left a scratch."

Janklow nodded approvingly. "Just so. We might conclude from a scratch of that depth that our thief either has long, thick fingernails or…"

"Wears a ring," I finished, feeling more exhilarated with each discovery.

"So we are looking for a person of considerable height – a man, most likely – who wears a ring. As I see it, two questions emerge." Janklow lifted one finger. "Firstly, who of that description would wish to steal the painting?"

As I thought about what sort of person our culprit could be, Imogen blurted out "Anyone who wanted to make a lot of money," as if the answer were obvious.

"Ah yes, Miss Humphreys, the motive of money often comes into play. But we must weigh it up with the second question: Who would wish to steal the painting, *and*," he lifted a second finger, "*why* replace it with this particular, unknown picture?"

I had been asking myself the same two questions for the past two days, but as I had not succeeded in coming up with any answers, I kept quiet.

Imogen spoke up again. "Maybe the thief hoped no one would notice?"

Janklow considered this. "Possible," he answered. "But that implies our crook is an idiot. This does not appear to be the work of an idiot; therefore, I believe the choice is significant."

I hadn't thought of it like that before. "So, you think

whoever did it was trying to send a message about Mr. Webb?"

Janklow tapped his nose. "My thinking precisely, Miss Watson."

I bit my lip, trying not to beam at his praise.

Janklow continued. "I've asked Mr. Webb to provide me with a list of all of his rivals, enemies and patrons. Meanwhile, I've asked my contact, an art dealer by the name of Mortimer, to go digging through some more obscure archives from London's lesser-known galleries." He paused to consult his pocketwatch. "If we leave now, we should be right on time to meet him. I am hoping he will have some tasty little morsel of information to offer us. Shall we?"

I could have walked on air. Collecting clues, meeting agents, collaborating with a real London detective. *If only Charlie could be here to see me now,* I thought as I followed Janklow through the cathedral doors and watched him fix his bowler hat on again. This was the stuff Charlie and I used to pretend in our make-believe detective games. Now it was real, and I was right where I wanted to be: in the thick of it.

16

THE GAME IS ON

It was a short walk down Fleet Street back to Lincoln's Inn Fields. Inspector Janklow led us to a poky pub behind the Royal Courts of Justice called the Seven Stars. The place was packed with men dressed in black robes and white wigs. Through the fumes of their cigars, the strange sight of a black cat wearing a white ruff collar caught my eye as it paced along the bar and occasionally rubbed up against a drinker. As I watched it, a startlingly loud sneeze erupted from somewhere behind.

Janklow held up a finger. "I dare say that's our man."

Sure enough, Janklow followed the sound of the sneezes and forged his way to a table in a private little bay. There sat Dobbs and Betsy, accompanied by a funny-looking little balding man. He wore round wire spectacles, and his thin moustache moved up and down like an inchworm with every twitch of his nose.

Seeing the Inspector approach, the man stuffed his handkerchief into his pocket and stood to shake hands with Janklow. The top of his glassy head did not even reach the Inspector's shoulder.

"Penrose Mortimer, at your service," he said, offering us each a firm, fast handshake.

"This head you see here," – Janklow spoke to Imogen and me, but referred to Mr. Mortimer's head – contains more specialist knowledge of the visual arts than all of London's libraries put together."

"Now now now, Inspector," the man said in a voice that made me think of Munchkin Land. "You really oughtn't exaggerate my talents. But as it happens," he paused and pulled out his handkerchief just in time to catch a stupendous sneeze. "Cats," he sniffled. "Where was I? Oh yes. I was going to say that I *did* manage to dig up some information on–"

He was interrupted again by a barmaid who swished up to the table, flashing a glinting, gold-toothed smile. "What'll you and your friends 'ave, Inspector?"

"Thank you, Bonnie. The usual sherry for me and, erm, tea for the young ladies?"

We nodded. Bonny swished off to the bar and we all turned eagerly back to Mr. Mortimer's information.

"As I was saying, it took a great deal of digging, but I *did* manage to find a record of the mysterious little painting in the end. I am astonished I knew nothing of it before, as it was exhibited at the Royal Academy in 1848, and is the work of the Academy's most promising student at that time."

I was on the edge of my seat to hear the name of the person, but Mr. Penrose Mortimer carried on in his squeaky, excited way.

"The reviews suggest that the painting caused quite a stir at the time, and several offers of purchase were made. But it never went up for auction, and the promising young artist tragically threw away his future in dissolute living. He disappeared from good society altogether."

"Who was he?" I asked, unable to wait another second.

Mr. Mortimer slid a piece of paper across the table towards the Inspector. Imogen and I both leaned in. It was a magazine clipping with a tiny engraving of the painting. The heading on the article read, 'Celebrated Round Table Artist Gabriel Webb Shows New Side with Latest Work, *On the Steps of St. Paul's.*'

After scanning the article, Inspector Janklow leaned back and crossed his arms over his chest. "Well, well, Penrose. Looks like you've pinpointed our culprit." That look came into his eyes, as if he were focused on some distant vision only he could see. "Rival brothers. Why, it all fits like clockwork! Gabriel had all the promise but lost it. He has suffered his brother's success all these years in silence, and it's driven him mad. So what does he do? He replaces Phineas's greatest work with a forgotten, overlooked one of his own. How very elegant."

I listened carefully to his deductions. It all made sense, I couldn't disagree; but a heavy feeling of dread outweighed the excitement of discovery. Cautiously, I voiced my concern. "But if no one has seen Gabriel Webb in years, how do we find him?"

"Ah, Miss Watson," Inspector Janklow surfaced from his far-off place and looked me keenly in the eye. "Mr. Mortimer never said that Gabriel Webb had not been seen. Only that he had disappeared from *good* society. In this city, *good* society is but one stone in a thousand to turn over."

"But what if he's not *in* London anymore?" I asked.

Janklow tapped his nose with a wry smile. "Leave it to me, Miss Watson. I'm like a hound when it comes to sniffing out criminals. There is no distance too great for this nose of mine to follow."

A DENSE MIST had fallen on the dark London streets when we left the Seven Stars. Janklow bid us goodnight and turned towards his office. I could easily imagine him, elbows rested on his immaculate desk, his fingertips lightly touching, stewing over the case through the long night.

As tired as we all were from the day's business, there was now so much to think about. The three of us – Dobbs, Imogen and I – could talk of nothing but Gabriel Webb on the walk back to the Misses Turveys'.

"Do you think he knew about the paints he used? That they were..." Imogen stopped short when I gave her a look and raised my eyebrows towards Dobbs. He was listening carefully to every word. "Special?" she finished.

"Wha's so special 'bout 'em?" Dobbs asked. "Paints is paints, ain't they?"

We both pretended not to hear the question.

"The one thing we can be almost sure of is that he got the paints from Ramona, one way or another." I said.

"Then we're one giant leap closer to solvin' it!" Dobbs's impish face was full of excitement as it moved in and out of the lamplight. "We know who dunnit now. All we 'ave to do is find Gabriel, and I'll bet we find your missin' lady."

"Yeah, simple," I said a little more flatly than I meant to. In one way, he was right. We had taken a giant leap forward by unmasking the thief. But we had gained another missing person in the process, which felt like two giant leaps backwards.

We carried on talking as we turned onto Long Acre. I noticed that, except for the odd cab, the street was dead quiet now the dark had chased home the merchants and shoppers ... all except for one lone figure leaning against a lamppost just across the street from the hostel. The lamp's light flooded over him, leaving his face in shadow, but revealing a stunted, hulking shape in a brown, battered trench coat. The shadowy figure spat noisily, and Betsy began to growl deep in her throat.

My heart jumped into *my* throat. I reached out and pulled Dobbs closer to whisper in his ear. "Don't look now, but there's a man across the street. Do you recognise him?"

Dobbs pretended to bend down and lace up his shoe, in the meantime managing a glance towards the still, watching figure.

He stood up and leaned in close for Imogen and me to hear. "I don't know 'im, but I know *of* 'im. Name's Tobias Wix."

"Tobias Wix?" Imogen shot a glance over Dobbs's head. "What's that ape doing here? You don't think he's following us?"

"'Ow do you two know 'im?" Dobbs asked in a tone of surprise.

"The night we met you, he tried to steal Imogen's

purse," I explained. "Not the best introduction. Let's talk inside the gate," I urged, pushing it open.

I felt a little better with the gate between us and Wix, but I could still feel his invisible eyes watching. Betsy could too. She kept up her deep-throated rumbling.

"What do you know about him?" I asked Dobbs.

"Not much. He's known in unsav'ry circles as 'the Gargoyle'."

"I can see why," Imogen muttered.

Dobbs shook his head. "Not on account of his looks. It's cos he's done time for burglin' churches. Rumour is 'e used to travel with the circus as a trapeze flyer. Got a real head for heights wot 'elps 'im climb up church towers, see. 'E 'angs off 'em just like an ol' stone gargoyle. And 'e's got the strength to climb back down again with church valuables. You know–" He scratched his head. "Candlesticks and the like."

"The Gargoyle," I mouthed with a quick glance across the street. Yes, I could just about picture that figure scaling a church tower, monkey-like; the thought made me shiver. But, in an attempt to reassure myself as much as Imogen, I said, "See, Im. He's probably just waiting to go burgle a church. I doubt he even remembers us."

"Either way," Dobbs said, standing to his full height, "you don't need to worry. I'll be 'ere to look after you tomorrow. Only..." He snapped his fingers. "I forgot. Bess 'n' me is back to shoe blackin' in the morning. Inspector's orders. But I can come just after," he added eagerly.

Imogen huffed. "We *can* leave the house by ourselves, you know."

Dobbs's eyes dropped. "Course you can, if you like."

He rubbed his nose with his sleeve. "Just thought, as we're in this mystery-solvin' tomfoolery togever, I might…" he trailed off, turning as if to go.

"Dobbs," I blurted. He turned around hopefully. "I thought I'd go looking for my notebook tomorrow in the daylight. You know, retrace our steps from this morning. It would be really great if you could help, seeing as you'll remember the roads better than I will."

He stood upright and made a saluting gesture. "You can count on me, Miss. I'll be 'ere when the clock strikes noon."

As soon as he closed the gate behind him, Imogen grabbed my arm. "Come on, Katie. Let's not hang around to find out what that gargoyle person is up to. Especially now our bodyguard has gone," she added with a roll of her eyes.

When we were safe in our room, I peered out the dormer window. "He's gone," I announced with huge relief. Despite what I'd said before, I could not help feeling that Wix's appearance outside our lodgings was more than just coincidence.

17

A HAIRY SITUATION

From his city roost, the rooster crowed loud and clear. I opened one eye, surprised to find pale light spilling in through our little dormer window. I hadn't slept well. Dozens of questions about Gabriel Webb, the magic painting hanging in St. Paul's and the disturbing appearance of Wix outside the hostel had churned around in my head for what felt like hours until I finally fell into a fitful sleep.

Reluctantly opening the other eye, I tossed off the blanket and dragged myself out of bed and over to the window.

"Where's all that light coming from?" Imogen groaned, pulling the blanket up over her eyes.

I peered out across the chimney pots, glistening in the morning mist. Most of the snow had melted off the rooftops. The air looked cleaner now after yesterday's rain, and somewhere behind a veil of white mist, the sun was making a valiant effort to shine through. The pigeons on the window ledge were making the most of its rays, happily cooing as they preened their feathers. *That's just what I need to clear my head*, I thought. *Fresh air.*

"Let's go for a walk," I said brightly.

"Ugh," was the reply from under the blanket. But after some coaxing, Imogen got up. We dressed in our old charity clothes, ready to greet our first sunny, Victorian winter's day.

Covent Garden Market teemed with more activity than ever; even the sun's half-hearted rays had brought the crowds out in double. Imogen linked her arm through mine, and together we strolled past the market stalls, newspaper boys, flower girls with their shoulders draped in greenery, each shouting to be heard over the others.

I barely heard a single one of them. The brisk, sunny air was doing its magic. My mind felt less rusty now as it turned over all our discoveries from the day before.

"What I don't understand," I mused out loud, "is how Phineas didn't recognise the *On the Steps of St. Paul's* as his brother's. He must have seen it before. Do you think it's possible he just forgot about it?"

I glanced at Imogen. She clearly hadn't heard a single word I'd said. Her attention was turned longingly towards the market stalls piled high with fresh-baked bread, cheeses, and steaming pies.

"I'm so hungry, Katie," she groaned. "I honestly don't think I can bear to eat another one of those hard buns from the hostel. They just make me hungrier than I was before eating them."

I couldn't disagree. I had been grateful for the buns at the start of each day, but they were hardly manna from heaven.

I stood still, thinking. "There must be some way we can make a little money. Besides, we need to pay for our room at some point." I bit my lip, my eyes roving the market for some inspiration.

Meanwhile, Imogen plopped down on a little stool beside a Punch and Judy theatre.

"I'd sell my hair for a hunk of cheese right now."

"Really?" I asked. I had just spotted a wagon parked outside the pavilion, the sign over its curtained door hand-painted with the words WE BUY LADIES' HAIR.

"I swear I would."

"Well here's your chance. Look."

It had only been a joke, but, turning to look, Imogen got to her feet. "I have been considering shorter hair." And she made off towards the wagon.

"Im, wait!" By the time I caught up to her through the chock-a-block maze of wagons and carts, it was too late. She'd climbed the steps of the wagon and disappeared behind the curtain. I waited, horrible images of giant shears and a hairless Imogen haunting my mind.

I was wondering what I should do when I heard hysterical laughter behind me. I spun to see who was making the commotion and found myself facing a makeshift shed. "Oh," I said, remembering Dobbs's description of his sleeping quarters. "I bet…"

I approached the half-open stall door and stuck my head inside. The laughter, it turned out, had been the braying of a mule.

"Hello, Samson," I said, letting the mule sniff my hand before reaching up to stroke his stiff ears. "I'm Katie. We have a mutual friend. Your flatmate, Arty Dobbs."

Samson let out an ear-splitting bray.

"Shush up, ya one-eyed imbecile!" A drunken, tattily dressed old man stumbled over and kicked the side of the shed.

"It was my fault," I said as the man slid his back down the side of the shed until he lay on the ground with an upturned bottle held to his lips.

Full of indignation, I patted Samson's nose and gave him a reassuring smile. "Never mind. If anyone's an imbecile–"

"Katie?" I whirled around. The hair wagon's curtain was pulled back and Imogen was looking for me in the crowd. She spotted me and ran over. "What do you think?" she asked, shaking out her now chin-length blonde hair. The barber, still holding the long braid he'd recently snipped from Imogen's head, appeared behind her. "There you are, Miss." He held out his hand and dropped several gold coins into Imogen's palms. "Three sovereigns."

Imogen dropped the coins into her coin purse and patted it with satisfaction.

"How much is that worth?" I asked, relieved she had come out of the wagon in one piece.

"Not sure exactly," she answered. "But there was a woman in there with her daughter whose hair got only two sovereigns, and *she* said they'd take it and buy enough wool and boots to dress her seven children."

I gawked.

"I think it's safe to say we can afford to pay the Misses Turvey *and* buy a substantial feast with three sovereigns."

"You're the mathematics whiz. My only request is

apples," I said as Imogen took my arm and yanked me towards the food stalls.

The first thing she did was buy a basket from one of the many ladies balancing stacks of them on their heads. She proceeded to fill it with hot rolls, a giant chunk of cheese, dried apricots, baked potatoes, a jar of blackberry preserves and two bouquets of flowers, one for the Misses Turvey and the other for Mrs. Janklow to thank her for Christmas dinner. Finally, I picked out three of the biggest apples I could find.

"This is going to be the beggar's feast of a lifetime," Imogen said, happily biting into a plump apricot and handing another to me. "Though," she rolled her eyes, "I suspect we won't have long to eat it before Dobbs turns up wanting to chaperone us."

"He's not coming 'til noon," I said, then thought. "What time is it anyway?"

"Don't know. But that's just what we need." Imogen gave her coin purse a shake. "A watch." She looked around. "Excuse me. Yes, you." She spoke to one of the young men selling newspapers. "Any idea where I can buy a watch for a decent price?"

The young man removed his cap and scratched his head. "I know the place, Miss. There's a watchmaker on Cecil Court. Carry on down Long Acre, hang a left on St Martin's Lane. You'll find the place on your right in a wink."

Before setting off for the watchmaker, I asked Imogen to wait for me while I ran back to the shed. The gruff old man snored on the ground, so I went ahead and fed Samson all three apples.

"What was that about?" Imogen asked through a mouthful of cheese when I re-joined her.

"Just a gift for a friend."

She shrugged, and we set off down Long Acre, basking in the pale winter sunlight and the joy of sweet, juicy apricots as we walked. Just as the paper boy had promised, we found Cecil Court in no time, a narrow alley lined with shops and hanging signs.

"Ah. That must be the one." Imogen pointed at an iron sign in the shape of the cogs, wheels and hands of a clock. As we approached, I read the words painted on the window.

Salomon & Botts, Makers of Clocks, Watches & Mechanical Toys since 1620

"Salomon & Botts," I repeated out loud. "Where have I heard that before?" I searched my memory and gasped, causing Imogen to start and choke on the cheese. "Salomon and Botts was engraved on the back of Phineas Webb's pocketwatch!"

"Oh great," Imogen said, sputtering and wiping her watering eyes. "If Phineas Webb shops here, we'll never be able to afford it."

"No, but don't you see?" I said, patting her on the back. "Whoever made that watch knows Ramona's song. Maybe knows Ramona herself! Imogen, you're a genius!"

"Thanks, but what did *I* do?"

I laughed with the giddiness of our good luck. "You led us here!" And linking arms, I reached for the door knob. "It's a good thing you're crazy enough to go cutting off all your hair."

. . .

A *CUCKoo, CUCKoo* greeted us as we crossed the threshold into the cramped but extraordinary little shop. I looked up to see the little wooden bird in the cuckoo clock above the door. It flapped its mechanical wings and *cuckooed* again before retreating back inside its miniature house. The shop was dark with low, sloping ceilings; but where shafts of light found their way through the windows, they illuminated shelves upon shelves of impossibly-detailed toy theatres, marionettes, music boxes and clocks of all shapes and every colour. My eyes could have gone on exploring those shelves all day, but they were drawn away by the footsteps on the stairs behind the counter.

A willowy old man with wispy white hair and a wisp of white beard, as if he'd just come down out of the clouds, stooped over the counter. His bright blue eyes twinkling behind half-moon spectacles.

"How might I serve you?" He spoke hoarsely and with a heavy accent.

"I'd like to buy a watch," Imogen said. "Nothing fancy. Just something simple."

The old man nodded and turned to the back wall of shelves lined with little boxes. "Shoo. Shoo, Häxa." He waved his hand at a grey kitten slinking along the shelf. "She looks for mice," he said, returning with a box of mismatched pocketwatches.

As Imogen began to rummage through them, I struck up conversation. "Do you make the watches yourself?" I asked casually.

He smiled and, taking a rag from his pocket to clean his glasses, answered, "Oh yes. The Salomon family has been making clocks for hundreds of years. The best in Switzerland."

"So *you're* the Salomon in Salomon and Botts?" I tried to sound innocently inquisitive, the way Imogen always managed to do so convincingly.

"Ah, that was my father. He brought our Swiss clocks to London and partnered with a famous toy theatre maker by the name of Botts. And so, there you have it."

I nodded. "Mr. Salomon–"

"Please, call me Jacques."

"Jacques, I saw the most extraordinary musical pocketwatch recently, and it had your name on it. I wonder if you might remember it?"

"Wait, wait." He picked up a small trumpet and held it to his ear. "Now, you were saying about this pocketwatch?"

I described the watch, its little canary bird and the sad, sweet song it sang in every detail I could remember. When I finished, he lowered the little ear trumpet.

"I know this watch," he said.

"You do?" Imogen had left off rummaging through the box and leaned forward eagerly.

"Oh yes, I recollect it perfectly." His eyes sparkled behind his spectacles. "It was one of a kind, made to order, though I was not the one to make it. You see, the watch you describe is very old... though not quite so old as me, perhaps." He chuckled wheezily. "But I do remember a young man bringing it to me for mending."

"Oh yes, that must be the one." I was almost breathless with excitement. "It looked as though the case had been cracked and put back together. How long ago would you say you mended it?"

He scratched the side of his head, making his wispy hair feather out like cotton candy. "Years ago," he said at last. "Before the hairs on my head turned white, I think."

My rising excitement took a plunge. "Oh," I said. "I don't suppose you still remember what the young man looked like?"

"But of course, I do. How could I forget? He was, after all, quite famous then. He and his young painter friends were going to revolutionise art forever, as I recall. Yes, young Gabriel Webb."

Imogen and I looked at each other, confused. "Do you mean Phineas Webb?" I asked.

Mr. Salomon wheezed out another chuckle. "No, no. I may be losing my marbles, but I'd know Phineas Webb as well as everyone else in this city. No, the young man who brought me the canary pocketwatch was Gabriel, Phineas's lesser-known brother. A very quiet, soft-spoken young man. But very polite, as I recall... Ah, and he had a lame leg."

I was gobsmacked. "Gabriel? But–"

Whatever question I meant to ask was interrupted by a *cuckoo* as the door opened and heavy steps entered the shop behind us.

Imogen tensed but stared straight ahead. Without turning around, I felt the hair rise on the back of my neck. At the same time, the grey kitten screeched and dove from its shelf to skulk behind the counter. Mr. Salomon looked uneasy as he adjusted his spectacles on his nose and cleared his throat. "May I help you, sir?" he wheezed.

A thick, gnarly, dirty hand smacked down upon the counter. Instinctively, I jumped back and saw the very person I'd dreaded. Mr. Wix stood at my shoulder, his breath rasping, his ape-like shoulders hunched around his ears, his scarred face contorted in a hideous scowl directed at me.

I quickly looked away, trying to stay composed. "Thank you, Mr. Salomon." My throat had gone dry and I had to swallow before I could say another word. "We'll think about the watch and come back another time."

Mr. Wix's scowling eyes followed us to the door. We were out in a cat's wink, but not before I got a good look at his hand.

18

A MYSTERIOUS MESSAGE

*P*eeking out from behind a parked omnibus on St Martin's Lane, we watched Mr. Wix leave the shop. He glanced up and down Cecil Court, then pulled up his collar and walked briskly down the alley in the opposite direction.

"Thank goodness," Imogen whispered, relaxing the grip she had on my forearm. "Now, shall we go back and get that watch I wanted?"

I glared at her.

"I'm only kidding," she said with a nervous laugh. "Let's get back to our room before that creeper catches up to us again. Besides, I'm dying to dig into this cheese."

"You really think he's following us then?" I asked as we meandered our way back through the market stalls.

"*Of course* he's following us, Katie. What are the odds in a city of this size that we would just *happen* to keep bumping into him? That he would just *happen* to be hanging about outside our hostel? I don't know how he managed to follow us home without our noticing. Just the thought of it makes my skin crawl." She shivered.

I didn't like the image of a lurking, spying Wix on our trail any better than she did. "We should tell Janklow," I said, decidedly putting the image out of my mind.

"Hasn't he already gone to investigate that Gabriel Webb lead up in Lincolnshire?"

I had forgotten. A messenger boy had brought us a note from Janklow late last night informing us that he had tracked down one of the Round Table painters who, he hoped, might know something of Gabriel's whereabouts. The note said that he would leave on the nine o'clock train to Lincolnshire that morning. He hoped to bring us news by the next day.

The thought of Janklow being miles away made me uneasy, but I tried to put on a brave face. "We'll just have to tell him the minute he gets back."

"Yes, we'll tell him. But we don't need Janklow to tell us Wix is involved in this stolen painting business."

I stopped beside the frozen fountain in the market square and looked her in the eye. "What makes you think so?"

"Isn't it obvious? First of all," she held up her thumb, "when and where was the first place we ever saw him?"

"Near St. Paul's on the night of the theft," I admitted.

"Secondly, what reason would he have for following a couple of girls around London unless he suspected we were on his case? And third," she held up another finger, "didn't you hear what Dobbs said? The man has done time for burgling churches. For heaven's sake, he's the perfect suspect. I honestly can't believe we didn't see it before. Why are you shaking your head?"

"Can't be," I said. "Remember the mark on the wall at the crime scene? The person who hung that painting had to be tall. Wix looks strong enough to carry away a huge painting, but not tall enough to hang the replacement. *And* he doesn't wear any rings."

Imogen squinted dubiously. "How do you know that?"

"I looked at his hands back in Salomon & Botts."

She looked impressed but wasn't ready to give up her angle. "Well *you're* the detective, but I'd be willing to bet this entire basket of food it was Wix."

"And what about Gabriel Webb?" I challenged. "We know the painting is his, and now it turns out the pocket-watch was once his too. Seems to me that all the evidence points to him."

"I'm not saying he isn't behind it. The painting is his. That I accept. But what if he didn't act alone? After all, nobody's seen the man for years. Could be he's in hiding but still pulling the strings on some grand master scheme to get back at his brother."

We stopped beside a fountain. I perched on the edge, puzzling over Imogen's suggestion. As I did, my eyes happened to fall on a lame beggar beside the greengrocer's cart. A sign hung around his neck: *War in Africa left me with one leg. Please help.* With one hand, he held out his upturned cap for coins, and with the other he supported himself with a makeshift crutch.

"You know, Im, I think you might be right. What was it Mr. Salomon said about Gabriel Webb?"

"He said Gabriel was polite, quiet, and... oh! He said he was lame," she answered.

"Exactly. So he couldn't have performed the theft on his own. He had to have help."

"And that help had to be strong enough to carry the painting out of the building for him. Like Wix," she added smugly.

"And now," I said, feeling a fog was lifting, little by little, "somehow, Gabriel Webb has found out we're on his tracks and sent Wix to keep an eye on us."

Imogen nodded in an 'I told you so' way.

I stared at her, a mad idea dawning in my racing mind. "You know, if Wix is working for Gabriel Webb, he might just lead us to his hiding place."

"You mean you want *us* to follow Wix?" Imogen gave me a look as if she thought I'd finally cracked. "You are joking? May I remind you that *he* is the one following *us*? Have you ever tried following someone who's trying to follow you at the same time? I'm pretty sure you just end up going in circles."

"We'll simply have to outsmart him," I said. My imagination was hard at work, painting pictures of knocking on Gabriel Webb's door and demanding he tell us where he had got Ramona's paints ... of finding her at last... of Inspector Janklow praising us for cracking the mystery all on our own...

The pictures evaporated as the church bells began to chime in the hour. We listened, counting the ten gongs of the clock.

"I can't outsmart anyone on an empty stomach,"

Imogen said, decisively hoisting her basket over her shoulder. "Let's eat now and make a plan after."

"Agreed." I jumped up, taking a quick detour to drop a few shillings in the lame beggar's cap on our way.

As Imogen pushed open the gate of the Hostel for Girls of Good Character, she said over her shoulder, "I'd still like to know why Phineas Webb lied about getting that watch from a pawn shop."

My mind had been so preoccupied, I hadn't thought of that. "Maybe he's just ashamed to say he got it from his good-for-nothing brother," I offered. "Same reason he's forgotten Gabriel's painting. Sounds like Phineas has tried to forget he has a brother at all."

"Sad, isn't it?" she said as we climbed the stairs to the door. "Those two looked like such good friends in the photograph. I wonder what happened?"

The moment we entered the house, Effie Turvey came bustling up the corridor.

"My dears, I suppose you've been out taking the fresh air this morning? How lovely." She folded her hands and beamed at us a moment.

"Oh, uh, yes, and I've just got a letter from my father," Imogen said, setting down her basket of food and fishing out her coin purse again. "Here you are, Miss Turvey. He's sent some payment for our stay so far, and says to thank you from the bottom of his heart for looking after us so well."

"Oh! Bless his soul." She tucked the coins into her own little purse and dabbed her eyes with her lilac handkerchief. "You must tell him it is our greatest joy to feed and care for such dear lambs, just as our Lord would have us do."

She beamed after us as we started up the stairs. When we were halfway up to the first landing, she exclaimed, "Oh! I nearly forgot!" and taking an envelope from her pocket, she bustled up the stairs after us. "This was left for you about half an hour ago, Katie dear."

"Oh." I looked at my name written in lavish calligraphy on the front. "But who delivered it, Miss Turvey?"

"Oh, just a messenger boy, my dear. Didn't say on whose errand he'd come, I'm afraid."

I waited until we reached our room to tear open the envelope.

"Well? Who's it from?" Imogen asked through a mouthful of bread as she unpacked the basket and laid our feast out on the bed.

I shook my head, my eyes scanning rapidly down the page. I flipped it over to check the back. "It doesn't say."

Imogen frowned. "Well what *does* it say?"

"Someone's found my detective notebook. Listen to this:

I have in my possession a notebook inscribed with your name and address. If it is of any value to you, come to the Taxopholite Club in Regent's Park at 11 AM today and await me at the pavilion. I will be happy to restore it to its rightful owner.

Yours respectfully–

"But there's no signature," I said, flipping the note over to inspect the back once again.

Imogen frowned. "Why make you go all that way to get it? Why not just send it with the messenger?"

I stared at the elegant penmanship, wondering what kind of person's hand had written it. "I don't know. How far of a walk is it to Regent's Park?"

Imogen shrugged. "About half an hour."

"Then if we leave right away, we should get there in plenty of time to find this place."

"But..." Imogen gazed longingly at the bread and cheese she'd taken such care to set out. "What about Dobbs? You told him we'd meet him here at noon."

"We'll be back by noon," I said, smirking at her pretend concern for Dobbs. "And we'll have the feast then, I promise."

She bit her lip, unable to tear herself away from the spread.

"I can go on my own, Im, if you'd rather stay here."

She sighed and reached for her hat. "Don't be silly," she said flatly. "I'm coming with you." She shoved the hat back onto her head, then stopped, sprinted back to the bed, snatched up a roll and stuffed an enormous bite into her mouth. Returning, she pulled the door closed behind us with a last, agonised look back.

19

THE CAPTAIN'S CAPTIVES

I left a message with Agatha Turvey to tell Dobbs where we'd gone in case we were a few minutes late getting back. I wished he had come with us on our errand. We were having no luck at all finding the Taxopholite Pavilion, as neither Imogen nor I knew what that word meant, and had to ask a constable patrolling the park if he had any ideas. He pointed us in the right direction and we found ourselves, as it turned out, at an archery club.

The pavilion was a sort of clubhouse where the archers took tea between shooting rounds. Imogen glanced around at the well-dressed ladies and gentlemen clinking their china teacups and laughing as they shared stories about past fox hunts. "This mystery person must be posh. Of course," she added ominously, "that hardly means he or she isn't evil."

It didn't feel like the sort of place a malicious plotter would choose to set a trap. "They probably didn't want to entrust the notebook to the messenger is all," I said, trying to sound optimistic.

"Or they were determined to meet the famous Katie Watson for themselves," Imogen said with a smirk. She glanced at a grandfather clock in the corner. "It's not yet eleven. Fancy a cup of tea?"

I couldn't deny her one cup of tea after I had dragged her away from her beloved feast, so we took a table and ordered a pot of Ceylon and two slices of ginger cake. As soon as the waiter filled our cups and stepped aside, a little red-headed boy appeared in his place. He wiped his nose on his sleeve, smudging dirt over his freckled cheeks, and stared at us blankly.

"Hello," I said uncertainly.

"Is one of you a Miss Katie Watson?" He belted out the question so loudly, several tea drinkers turned to gawk in our direction.

"I am," I said quietly, hoping he'd pipe down.

"Was told to give you this," he said just as loudly, and pulled my notebook out from his ragged little jacket.

"Thanks, but *who* told you to give it to me?" I whispered, taking it from him and rubbing the smudges off the cover with my napkin under the table.

The boy shrugged. "Dunno."

Imogen tried. "Can't you remember anything about the person who gave it to you?"

"I runs lots o' errands for lots o' folk. Can't rightly 'member one from the next, Miss."

We looked at each other, not sure what to make of this odd situation. The boy continued to stand there, as if waiting for something.

"Was there something else?" I asked.

He held out his grubby hand.

"Oh, sorry. Im, could you...?"

She clicked her tongue. "Not the most helpful service, but I suppose..." She opened her coin purse and placed a couple of coins in his hand. It must have been a better tip than he was used to getting. He stared wide-eyed at his palm, then a snaggle-toothed smile lit up his face. "Bless ya, Miss!" he shouted before scampering away, just like a miniature Dobbs.

"Well that was strange," Imogen said.

"Uh-huh." I was already rifling through my notebook. There was no damage that I could see. All the pages seemed to be intact. I flipped to the back cover and pulled open the little pocket. The photograph of the two young Webb brothers was still there. I took it out and placed it on the table between Imogen and me. Leaning in for a closer look, I spotted something I hadn't noticed before. It was just as Mr. Salomon had said! Gabriel Webb had one arm braced around his brother's neck; the other was supported by a cane.

"Katie..." Imogen was tapping my arm over and over.

"What?" I said, a little annoyed at the interruption. But as I looked up, I saw for myself. Mr. Wix paced back and forth beneath the branches of a yew tree, like a prowling beast, just outside the pavilion porch.

Imogen growled in her throat. "How did he find us here?"

I stuffed the photograph back into the journal pocket and threw it into my bag. "There must be a way out through the back." I cast about for an alternative door but found none. "We'll have to try the kitchen. There's bound to be a way out through there."

I watched until the waiter reappeared with a tray of tea things. "Quick!" I waved Imogen to follow me as I bee-lined, head down, for the kitchen.

There it was. The kitchen door was already open. I could see the frosted grass on the other side.

"May I help you?"

I froze and stood up. A square-shaped, flush-faced cook with a rolling pin in hand was giving us the evil eye.

I opened my mouth, but Imogen was faster. "We've just come to give our compliments to the chef. Marvellous cake." She gave me a shove, and we carried right on out the door, leaving the cook in speechless surprise.

Once out on the lawn, we sprinted towards the first cover we saw (a row of hay stacks acting as archery targets), jumped behind one nobody was using, and peered around.

"Katie, I hate to ask…"

"What?" Imogen's squeamish tone made me uneasy.

"You don't think Wix could've stolen your notebook without your noticing it, do you?"

I gulped. It was a chilling thought, and one I preferred not even to imagine. "Well I'm sure he didn't write the letter," I asserted, mostly to make myself feel better. "There's no way his penmanship is that perfect."

"But Gabriel Webb might have written the letter," she persisted. "Wix just did the stealing."

I didn't answer. If Imogen was right, we were dealing with a man who was as dangerous as he was hideous. A man who could make even his hulking presence invisible and seemed always to be lurking not far off. Yet, as much as I wanted to be rid of him, to be running in the opposite direction, this man was our best shot at solving this mystery once and for all.

"He's moving!" I whispered hoarsely. "He's looking in at the pavilion window! Oh, oh, he's leaving. Quick!"

Imogen groaned but followed. We scampered from haystack to haystack until we reached the last one in the row.

"He's taking the path around the pond," I whispered.

We followed at the safest distance we could manage while still keeping an eye on Wix's back, scurrying behind trees, shrubs, a gardener's wheelbarrow, boarded-up lemonade stands, any cover we could find, never letting Wix out of our sight. A time or two, he turned suddenly as if sensing he was being followed, and then we ducked down low and held our breath until he carried on his way.

We followed him right across Regent's Park when, finally, he reached the eastern gate.

Beyond the park gates, we found ourselves in a very different part of town. Long, straight rows of tall, sooty brick buildings all stacked on top of one another loomed up on either side and stretched as far as the eye could see. As we walked along, passing door after door, sometimes a smudged, sad face peered out at us from a grimy window. A few barefooted children were following their ringleader in a hunt after a rat, but they gave up the chase to watch us when we passed.

Imogen, grimacing from a foul, fishy smell in the air, whispered, "Do you think he's gone inside one of these houses?"

I stopped walking and squinted to try to see further up the long street. My eyes scanned the bare heads of men and women and finally landed on the familiar hat. "There!" I said. "He's just turned right behind that post box!"

We picked up our pace and ran to the place where he had disappeared. It was a dark, narrow, drippy alleyway with ropes of soggy laundry hung between the two buildings on either side like strange, ghostly bunting. The eerie cry of seagulls echoed through the brick tunnel like a warning.

We looked at each other, clearly feeling the same strong reluctance to enter.

With a deep breath, I asked, "Ready?"

Imogen plugged her nose. "Ready."

We picked our way through the alley, trying not to think about the squidgy, smelly substance beneath our feet. Though it was too dim to see them, the coughing and muttering of people huddled between crates and barrels followed our steps. I gripped Imogen's hand and walked more briskly.

At last, the gulls' cries grew louder and pale light crept into the alleyway. We reached the other end and both breathed in the fresh air. We had come out onto a busy towpath beside the canal. A little way up the path, men were driving mules to pull a barge of goods along the canal. They were stopped, waiting at a lock for the water to fill up. A group of boys leaned over the bridge that spanned the lock, tossing stones down into the canal, laughing and throwing more each time the men working the barge shouted at them to stop.

But there was no Wix.

"Bet he went over the bridge," Imogen said.

We crossed over, ignoring the gawking stares and jeers of the rock throwers. The other side of the canal was a wharf like the one we'd visited in King's Cross with Dobbs. It was covered by a timber frame, and littered with the same barrels, crates, rope and other shipping knick-knacks.

We wandered aimlessly between the stacks of crates that seemed to go on and on. There was no sign of anyone, and quite frankly, it was the last place I wanted to meet Wix. I turned to Imogen. "I don't think he came this way. We might as well turn ba–"

Her scream drowned out every other sound. I didn't even hear the heavy feet hit the ground as Wix dropped from a beam overhead. But I felt his landing shake the ground right behind me and swung around to see his gnarled, scarred face contort into a wicked leer.

"Lookin' for me are ye, darlin'?"

I turned to run, but his hand caught my arm and wrenched me back. Imogen grabbed hold of my free hand and yanked while I tried to free my other hand; but with every pull, his gorilla-like grip only tightened all the more.

"You can have my purse," she shouted. "Whatever you want, just let her go!"

He threw back his head and laughed. "Your purse?" He laughed again. "If I'd wanted your purse, I'd 'a had it an 'undred times by now. It's your 'eads I'm after."

"Our heads?" Imogen screeched. I felt tears pouring down my face from the pain in my arm. Suddenly, he jerked it, bringing me close to his leering face and rotten breath, "Tha's right. You got a bounty on your 'eads. A *very* 'andsome bounty."

I leaned away from the putrid breath, and, at the same time, heard a loud, echoing *crack!* The leer dropped from Wix's face. He looked confused. His grip loosened. He swayed on the spot, and, next second, his eyes rolled up just before he stumbled over into a stack of crates, knocking them over.

Standing there, his walking stick braced in both hands, was Captain Nemo. His dog Alpheus was at his side, lips pulled back and teeth bared at Wix beneath the pile of crates.

"Quickly." Nemo lowered his stick and beckoned us to follow him.

I cast one glance at the pile under which Wix was buried and heard a terrible, rasping breath beneath them as they began to move. A hand rose up between the boxes, throwing one off to reveal a face that could freeze the sun.

That was enough to make me follow after Nemo who limped, as hastily as I think he could go, towards the canal where the *Bella Ramona* was moored, her chimney smoking in readiness.

He straddled the gap between boat and land, and held out his hand to us. "Come quickly. I'm no match for that monster." His voice was urgent.

I hesitated. We were trapped between two dangers. I had only a second to decide which was worse.

"You'll be safe. I promise," he said earnestly, reaching out his hand to me as if he understood my dilemma.

A mighty "*Argh!*" bellowed from behind. With a rush

of fear, I took the outstretched hand and leapt into the barge.

Within seconds, Nemo was drawing up the rope and pushing the *Bella Ramona* off from her mooring, and not a second too soon. Wix skidded up to the edge of the canal, teeth bared and chest heaving with anger.

Imogen grabbed my hand. We had escaped one pursuer, but only to put ourselves at the mercy of another. For better or for worse, we were prisoners aboard the *Bella Ramona* now.

20

MR. WIX'S MASTER

The Captain steered in silence from the outer deck. Neither Imogen nor I spoke. Even Billy Bones seemed to realise it was no time for banter and kept his chatter to the occasional "Shiver me timbers!"

I stood by the portal window and glanced over my shoulder at Imogen. She sat in the armchair in front of the wood stove. Alpheus's chin rested on her knees, and she stroked his slick black head in a sort of trance. I wondered if she was in shock.

I turned back to the window, looking out for signs of where the Captain was taking us... wondering if Wix would be able to follow... if *anyone* would be able to find us again.

It was some time before we reached a place where the canal forked, and Captain Nemo turned the *Bella Ramona* down a stretch of canal that branched off the main course. Soon, the London buildings gave way to pastures, and bare tree limbs hung out over the water. There were other houseboats moored there. Captain Nemo moored up alongside a row of them. It was as good a hiding place as any for a long boat.

Alpheus lifted his head at the sound of his master's footsteps and cane clunking down the steps and into the cabin. Some clattering noises followed in the back room, and Alph left Imogen to go and investigate. She pulled her feet up under her in the chair and shivered. I went over to sit on the rug beside her.

In a minute, Alph and Captain Nemo appeared in the doorway, Nemo struggling to balance a kettle and several mugs on a tea tray in one hand. I stared at him. Though he stooped under the boat's low ceiling, he was tall. My eyes travelled to his cane, then to his crippled leg. His right foot turned inward.

I got up to help him with the tea tray. Taking it from his hand, my eye caught sight of the ring on his smallest finger, the one he'd played with constantly when we last were aboard the *Bella Ramona*.

With a quick intake of breath, I looked up to find his stern eyes piercing into mine.

"You... you're Gabriel Webb."

I heard Imogen gasp and stir in her chair. I kept his gaze, waiting for his answer.

After a pause, his eyes dropped. "I was once. But I've been nobody for many years now." Then, pushing past me, he limped across the hearth rug, lowering himself with a grunt onto a stool in the corner behind the wood stove where he rubbed his leg as if it were in pain.

I set the tray down on the little tea table. "So this was all a trap. Wix chased us here so that we'd have no choice but to take your help. Although..." I recalled the blow with which he'd sent Wix tumbling and felt suddenly uncertain. "Why would you knock out your own hitman?"

"Why indeed, Miss Watson?" He smiled painfully. "If the evidence doesn't fit your assumption, you must assume that your assumption is incorrect."

I looked to Imogen who appeared not to understand him any better than I did.

"In other words," he said, seeing our looks of confusion, "you are quite wrong in thinking that I am associated in any way with Tobias Wix. Just as I was wrong to believe that *you* were."

I was completely taken aback. "Us? Associated with *him*?"

"Only now, in light of what happened back there, do I see that I was mistaken," he continued. "It seems we both of us misjudged the other. We might turn out to be on the same side after all."

Imogen seemed suddenly to awaken from her shock. "And just what side is that?" she demanded. "Last time we saw you, you tried to kidnap us. You're no better than Wix."

"Ah yes. I am sorry for that." His apology sounded genuine. "You see, as I've said, I suspected then that you had been sent to spy on me by the same person who sent Wix to break into my barge some weeks ago."

"Who would do that?" I asked.

"Can you not guess, Miss Watson? Think. What was the name I told you the first time we met?"

"Phineas? But he's your brother..." This new picture was so unexpected, I couldn't make sense of it. "Phineas sent Wix after us?"

He nodded with a bitter smile. "Wix is no more than a vulture waiting to gobble up the scraps that Phineas leaves behind."

"But I don't understand why Phineas would send him after *us*."

Imogen clasped her hand over her mouth. "Wix said something about a... a bounty on our heads." She looked sick.

"For the same reason he sent Wix after me," Gabriel answered. "I can only presume Phineas has reason to believe you know something you should not?"

I caught his eye and quickly looked away.

"Something," he persisted, "that might put Phineas and the world he's built for himself at risk. It isn't safe to know too much, Miss Watson. Ignorance is bliss, or haven't you heard?"

My head felt all in a muddle. Could Gabriel Webb be trusted? It was all beginning to make sense, what he said about Phineas, yet I still sensed that he wanted something out of me, just as he'd wanted those sketches. I was determined not to tell him anything about Ramona until I knew exactly what he was after... and why.

"There are some things I need to know," I said. "Like why you didn't tell us Phineas was your brother. Or why your barge is *really* called *Bella Ramona*. Or why you've been in hiding all this time, and–"

"Are these truly things you *need* to know, Miss Watson?" He interrupted. "We shall see. But just now you're aboard *my* ship, at *my* mercy, so if you don't mind, *I* shall be asking the questions."

I glanced at Imogen who was making a great effort to

keep her mouth shut while glaring at our rescuer with a mutinous look in her eye.

"You may drink your tea," he said with a sly smile, as if he found our mistrust amusing. His calmness infuriated me. I felt I was playing a game of cards with someone who knows he has the upper hand.

I poured a mugful of tea and handed it to Imogen, then poured myself one and took a sip.

Satisfied, he began. "First question. How did you come by that sketchbook?"

"I told you," I said. "It was a gift from Ramona. She's a relation–"

"It's a lie." He smiled as if he'd caught me in a corner. "Ramona has no family. They all died of yellow fever. Only she and her grandmother survived, and her grandmother died and left her on her own when she was just a girl."

I glared at him, angry but hungry to know more. "How do you know that?"

He raised his finger. "My turn to ask the questions, Miss Watson, remember? Now, if you're not Ramona's relation, what is she to you?"

I opened my mouth, but closed it again. If I told him the truth, he was sure to think I was lying. So I threw the question back. "Why do you want to know? What's she to you?"

"I'm asking–"

"I know. You're asking the questions." I could see he was getting impatient, but so was I. We weren't getting anywhere like this. "Look," I said. "I just want to find her... to help her. How do I know you're her friend? You could be her enemy? I'm not telling you any more until you tell me what you know about her."

His cool, calm demeanour was slipping away; he looked as though he were bottling something up. I expected him to refuse, or even shout. But instead, he let out whatever he'd been bottling up in a rush of breath until his head hung and his shoulders sagged. "I want to find her too."

Whatever I'd expected, I hadn't expected that. Since yesterday, I had been so sure that Gabriel Webb would be the key to Ramona, that if we found Gabriel – the man behind the mysterious magic painting – we would find her.

"Then you have no idea where she is either?" I asked, feeling like a bowling pin must feel when it's struck over.

He shook his head wearily.

"But what about your painting? *On the Steps of St. Paul's*? It was..." I caught Imogen's eye and realised I'd said too much? I had almost given away that we knew all about the painting's magic; and hadn't Gabriel just warned me, it was dangerous to know too much.

"What about that painting?" No doubt about it, his suspicions were raised.

"Well..." There was no way out of it now. "It was painted with Ramona's paints, wasn't it?"

His eyes narrowed beneath his thick, black furrowed eyebrows. "How could you know that?"

Imogen let out an exasperated sigh. "You might as well just tell him, Katie. We're already his prisoners. It's not as if we have anything to lose."

I wasn't so sure, but I decided to take the risk all the

same. I set my teacup down and pushed myself up to my knees. "Mr. Webb, it was your painting that..."– I struggled for the right words – "that brought Imogen and me here."

He studied me for a moment before answering. "The truth is, Miss Watson, I did not paint it. Ramona did. That is, she and her grandmother painted it together when Ramona was only twelve years old."

"But the auctioneer said you showed it at the Royal Academy–"

"That is because the Academy would not permit the true artist, a poor Cherokee girl, to exhibit. I intended to show the work as my own, and when the public received it with the admiration it was due, to expose Ramona as the true artist."

"That explains it," I said.

"Explains what?" He leaned forward and spoke slowly, giving weight to each word. "Where precisely have you come from?"

Imogen and I exchanged a look. We were defeated. It was time to come clean. "You were right," I said. "I'm not Ramona's cousin. But I wasn't lying when I said I was her relation. Ramona is my... my great-grandmother."

His face was unreadable. He searched my face as if trying to find something he had lost. When at last he spoke, his voice rose only just above a whisper. "Ramona had a child?"

I nodded. "A daughter. Ka-Ti."

"And," he stroked his beard nervously, "and Ka-Ti's father?"

"His name is Jim Weaver. He's a fur trader in America."

"And is he… a good man?"

I couldn't believe it. Gabriel's eyes were actually welling up.

"Very good," I assured him. Something occurred to me for the first time as I looked into his face. "You remind me of him a little," I said, and looked away as he wiped the first tear to fall down his cheek. Could it be that Gabriel had loved Ramona? That she had broken his heart?

I poured another mug of tea and offered it to him. "They miss her," I said gently. "Jim and Ka-Ti. They want her back. That's why we need to find her. To tell her they want her to come home. So if you know anything, anything at all that could help us…"

He looked up from his cup of tea, his face glistening, but set and determined. "I would do anything for her. I'll tell you all I know. It's a story known to only three people. Myself, Ramona and Phineas."

21

GABRIEL'S STORY

"When Ramona was only a baby, disease broke out in her village. All their loved ones were stricken down, but her grandmother fled with the little girl in hopes that she would be spared. Her grandmother, you see, had a rare gift. She was a painter. And in her younger days, her paintings had taken her across time and oceans. She painted a picture, and she and the little girl stepped through it. They travelled this way for years, place to place, time to time, selling their paintings and pigments.

"Then one day, when Ramona was a mere twelve years old, time ran out on her grandmother. She died, and Ramona was left to fend for herself. But her grandmother had foreseen the inevitable and had made arrangements. She gave her a book of sketches in which she had begun to paint the places and people Ramona could turn to… a way of retracing the trail they had blazed through time so that Ramona could find her way home, and always have help to turn to along the way.

"On one of their travels, they had met a young painter with two young boys. The younger of these was just a little older than Ramona, and the two had liked each other very much. So Ramona searched through her sketches and found the painting her grandmother had done of that painter's family in the year 1845.

"Next thing the young painter knew, a little girl with long black curtains of hair was standing at his door. Her grandmother had helped the man in hard times and sold him the paints that had made him his fortune; so, out of gratitude, he took the girl in.

"The younger son was delighted to have her for a companion. She had shown him kindness as no other child had ever done. He wasn't like other children, you see. He was born with a deformity. A club foot."

"You're the younger son? You grew up with Ramona?" I interrupted.

He nodded.

"Then so did Phineas."

"Yes, but as children, Phineas had very little to do with either of us. He was someone to look up to from a distance. He was older, handsome, talented, impressive. My mother's favourite son. I knew I could never compete. And I didn't care. I was Ramona's favourite, and that was enough for me. We were thick as thieves as children. When I became morose and hated myself because of my disability, Ramona could always cheer me with tales of her adventures with her grandmother. Of course, I believed them to be all made up, but I thought them wonderful all the same.

"Then we would look at her grandmother's sketches.

There was one she liked especially... a grassy meadow backdropped by a wood. It was wild and otherworldly, but oh, so peaceful.

"'This is home.' She would say. 'Elisi'– for that is what she called her grandmother – 'Elisi painted this when she was just a girl,' she would say. 'I'm going back there someday, to the year 1810.'

"And, of course, I would argue with her. 'It isn't *your* home. *This* is your home. And besides, you can't go back in time.'

"'Maybe I can,' she would argue back in her headstrong way.

"There was no winning an argument with Ramona. I would always concede in the end. 'Then take me with you when you go,' I would say, thinking it was all just a game... or a dream. Never imagining she really meant to go.

"But something always troubled me about Ramona's stories of far-off places in distant times. Oh, they were wonderful. But they were far too *real*. And the pictures she would paint in her grandmother's book, they too looked more like memories than fancies... as if she'd seen these things with her own eyes.

"As the years went by, the more I learned from my tutors and history books, the more I'd find I already knew from Ramona's stories and pictures. But how could she know so much? She was only a girl who had never been taught so much as to read. And yet...

"So one day, I asked her. I think she had longed to tell me the truth for years, had tried to tell me in subtle ways, though I had been too dense to understand. She told me her grandmother had given her a gift. The gift of paint. Her grandmother's paints were special. They had the power to grant the beholder the deepest desire of his heart. And what was more, she could paint doorways to the past.

"'Show me,' I told her, and pointed to her favourite picture. The meadow beside the forest. 'Take me there.'"

Gabriel paused. There was a faraway look in his eyes.

"And did she?" I asked.

His eyes slowly focused on mine. He smiled and nodded. "Everything changed for me that day," he said, the smile faltering. "When we were in that other place, I knew that nothing in the world mattered to me but her. That I loved her.

"My mother saw my feelings changing. She did everything she could to keep Ramona and me apart, but we had our secret world we could run away to where no one could find us. Finally, I was sent off to follow in Phineas's footsteps at the Royal Academy of Art. All I ever painted was her, in all the places that she loved."

His eyes wandered to the opposite corner of the cabin, landing on the unfinished painting of a black-haired girl in a meadow of wild flowers. "You were quite right," he said. "It is her."

"But," I hated to ask the question, because the next bit of the story was sure to be painful for him, "did something happen between you and Ramona? I mean, why did she leave?"

His eyes closed. "My father died, and my mother cast Ramona out. She had only ever tolerated her for my father's sake. Ramona came to me for help. Phineas and I had bought an apartment in Bloomsbury which we shared with a few of our fellow visionary art students. She became our muse, our housekeeper, the life of our home. She also took to painting, putting all of us to shame with her natural talents.

"But I had no desire to share her with the others, and especially with Phineas who had never taken any interest in her all of our childhood days. I did not trust him. I knew if ever he discovered the power of her paintings, he would wish to seize upon it for his own gain.

"I decided the time had come. I made a profession of love to Ramona and asked her to be my wife."

He paused and closed his eyes again. After a few seconds, I wondered if he would continue the story. Hesitantly, I asked, "And, what did she say?"

His eyes opened, but stared into the distance. "She refused me. She promised that she loved me more than anyone in the world, had always loved my goodness, my gentleness... said that I was her closest friend... her brother. She never wished to alter our relationship.

"I was furious. I knew how headstrong she could be. I would never change her mind. So, to my lifelong shame, I decided I would hurt her in return. I would show her how far from good and gentle I could fall. I threw myself head-first into every form of reckless living – ran up debts with gambling, drinking, brawling. Oh, I was very successful in causing her pain. You should have seen the way she would look at me when I'd come crawling into the house at some godless hour. She said she would have nothing to do with me until I stopped my self-destructive behaviour.

"One night, she confronted me, and I... I..." Gabriel choked, and cupped his hand over his lips. Tears were streaming down his face, but he took in a gulp of breath and made himself continue. "I had been drinking, and I became violent. I'd never strike her. Never. But I grabbed her arm and tore the necklace from her neck: a chain with a pocketwatch. It had belonged to her grandmother and played a song that she had sung to Ramona when she was a little girl. It was precious to her, and I threw it against the floor. I smashed it in two. The little bird inside could never again sing its song.

"I was horrified at what I'd done, sorrier than I could say. It woke me from my long stupor, but too late. She ran to her room, and when I followed her, she had gone. I found only her sketchbook. The painting of the meadow lay open, the grass rippling as if a wind had just passed through it. She had gone and left me behind."

After a long silence, I thought perhaps he had reached the end of the story. But that couldn't be the end. "And she never came back?" I asked.

Imogen, who had been hugging her knees into her chest all the while she listened to Gabriel's story, now unfolded herself. "That can't be the end," she protested. "You haven't explained how Phineas came to have the pocketwatch... or what he has to do with any of it."

Gabriel had been drying his face with his burgundy handkerchief, and he stuffed it into his pocket before answering. "I am sorry to say it, but that is not the end of the story, and Phineas's part begins where mine ends. But tell me, how do you know about the pocketwatch?"

I briefly explained how we had first seen the watch at Phineas's home and had recognised the canary's song, then how we had later discovered at Salomon & Botts that the watch had once belonged to him, Gabriel.

"And Phineas told you he got it from a pawn shop?" Gabriel shook his head with disgust. "You shall hear the rest of the story, including the truth about the canary pocketwatch."

22

PHINEAS'S PLIGHT

I filled our cups with tea, and we sat back as he began again.

"I waited for Ramona all that day and night, and the next day and night. She did not return. On the third day, feeling helpless and wanting to make amends for what I'd done, I had the idea to take the watch to Salomon & Botts to see if it could be repaired. I left it there, and when I returned home, I was confronted by my brother. He told me Ramona had come home. That I was not to speak to her... not even to see her. I was to leave his house that very day."

"Ramona wanted you to leave?" I asked, unable to believe she would cast out someone so dear to her, even after what he had done.

"I do not believe it was her wish," Gabriel said. "I have my theory..."

"Go on," Imogen urged him.

"I believe Phineas must have discovered Ramona just as she returned from the painting. Perhaps he blackmailed her. Perhaps he was very winsome and confidential and promised he would keep her secret safe. Either way, he saw to it that no one should have Ramona but himself. Not because he cared for her, but because he saw her as the key to his fame and fortune. You see, while we called our little artistic society the Round Table, it was always clear that Phineas considered himself our leader. He imagined himself ruler of some mystical kingdom of the past. When he discovered Ramona's talents, he would have seen a way of turning his dream into a reality.

"He turned all our other friends out of the house after I left. No one ever saw Phineas anymore, except coming to and leaving his exhibitions with a beautiful woman on his arm. Some called her his muse. He grew very famous and inconceivably wealthy. How he made his fortune almost overnight was a great mystery to everyone... except to me."

"How did he do it?" I asked.

"Ramona helped him to paint his masterpiece, *The Wedding Feast*. Critics said he must have travelled back in time to the Golden Age of Chivalry in order to paint such a life-like scene." Gabriel gave a mirthless laugh. "If they only knew how close they were to the truth, and who *really* deserved the praise."

I had to interrupt again. "But Ramona wouldn't stand for having her talents used just so Phineas could get rich. She wouldn't allow it. I'm sure of it."

"You are right," he said. "She did not like what she saw Phineas becoming."

"How do you know?" Imogen asked.

"She sent me a message saying she was sorry for all

that had happened. She had taken care to destroy all that remained of her special paints, and she was going home. She hoped I would forgive her. Me… forgive her." He rubbed his hand across his forehead.

"So that's when Phineas lost his fortune," I said, remembering the articles I'd read.

"Yes," Gabriel answered. "He nearly lost everything. He was hardly seen for many, many years. Then, a year ago, out of the blue, he announced he was producing a new series of paintings that would put all his past work to shame. Overnight, his fame and fortune returned a hundredfold. I had to know why, so I spied on him. Little did I know he had hired a spy of his own."

"Tobias Wix," I said.

Gabriel nodded. "To frighten me, he had Tobias discover where I lived. He broke into my barge and stole my two most prized possessions: *On the Steps of St. Paul's* and Ramona's pocketwatch.

"I was enraged. From then on, I watched Phineas all the more carefully, never letting Wix see me. One night, I got a cab and followed behind his carriage to St. Paul's Cathedral. I got out of the cab and watched in the shadows as Phineas alighted from his carriage, then helped a young woman alight. She wore a cape, but her hood was down, and I could see her face in the moonlight. Beyond a shadow of a doubt, it was Ramona!

"She looked just as I remembered her, unchanged by all the years, though Phineas and I had both gone grey. Then Phineas, Ramona and Wix approached the cathedral and disappeared, right before my eyes. I could not see where they had gone. But the carriage remained, and so I waited for them. After an hour, Phineas and Wix returned alone. I waited all night. Ramona never came. I watched Phineas like a hawk for weeks after that. Every few days, he would go to St. Paul's, disappear as he had before, then return shortly afterward, sometimes carrying a bag he hadn't had with him before. But never accompanied by Ramona."

He finished. My mouth was hanging open, speechless. Dread weighed stone-heavy in the pit of my stomach. "You don't think he would have…"

"No, Miss Watson. I don't believe Phineas killed her."

I let out a breath of relief.

"My brother may be a monster, but he is not a murderer. And besides, he only ever acts in his own interest. It is very much in his interest to keep Ramona alive. At least, that is what I say to myself for comfort. But I do believe it. After all, there is at least one good, alternative explanation for Ramona's disappearance."

The answer came to me. "She went through a painting," I said.

He nodded. "And we know of at least one painting in St. Paul's through which she might have travelled."

"*The Wedding Feast*," I answered.

Imogen stopped massaging her temples. "Wait a second. You said Phineas stole *On the Steps of St. Paul's* from your boat. Are you saying it was Phineas who hung it up in the place of *The Wedding Feast*? You had nothing to do with it?"

"You have the right of it, Miss Humphreys."

I was on my feet before I knew it. "We have to get word to Janklow right away." I was looking around as if I might find a telephone handy. "He thinks you did it. He's looking for you this very minute, and all the while Phineas is getting away with… with…"

"Yes, Miss Watson," Gabriel nodded. "You see the trouble, don't you? We don't know exactly what it is Phineas is up to. We have nothing to go on except our belief that Ramona has escaped through a magical painting. Imagine how that will sound to your inspector friend."

I gritted my teeth in frustration. "But if Phineas should disappear,"– my head reeled at the thought – "we'll never be able to find her. We should send word to him immediately."

I swung my shawl over my shoulders and made for the door, but Gabriel called out, "We are miles from London, Miss Watson. You have suffered an attack today and it is dark. You and Miss Humphreys should get some rest and wait for daylight.

"You can't keep us here," Imogen said, rushing to her feet, ready for a fight.

Gabriel held out his hands for peace. "You are not my prisoners, Miss Humphreys. Of course I cannot force you. I only advise you to wait. Get some rest. This is a dangerous business you are about, and you have enemies on your trail. I cannot navigate tonight, but tomorrow I will find a safe place to moor and accompany you to send a message to the inspector." He winced and massaged his leg.

Imogen looked at me with uncertainty. This whole business was so strange; everything I thought I knew had changed in the last few hours. We had discovered Gabriel Webb only to find that we'd been hunting the wrong man. Phineas had been the perpetrator all along… had had us followed, attacked by that monster Wix. Phineas had taken Ramona away.

I glanced at Gabriel. He had lit a pipe and silently stroked Alpheus's head. Hours ago, I'd never have trusted him, but the tears in his eyes when he had said how he loved Ramona were genuine. I believed what he said: he would do anything to help her.

"Ok," I said. "We'll get some rest and go with you tomorrow."

Gabriel told us where to find blankets and cushions and we settled down in front of the fire. Gabriel retired to the back cabin and left us to rest. Imogen still looked uneasy, but within minutes, her eyes closed and her breathing turned soft and steady. The barge rocked gently; the fire crackled. For all the thoughts spinning around in my head, in spite of the ache in my arm where Wix had gripped it, my eyelids could hold out no longer.

Galloping. Galloping. I am on horseback, riding across flat land. A stone tower covered in vines breaks the landscape. I approach, but I cannot reach the tower. A moat separates me from it. Then, I hear something. A beautiful, sweet, sad song. Before I know it, I am floating, weightless, up and up. The music grows more audible as I ascend. Then I stop.

I am peering into a tiny window, into the eyes of a beautiful lady. She looks at me and smiles as if she knows me, but her eyes are so sad. On her finger, a little golden canary is perched. The music is coming from its tiny beak.

It finishes its song and takes wing, flying for the window, for freedom! But it cannot get out. The window is barred. I cling to the bars and pull with all my might, but they will not budge. The canary returns to its perch on the lady's finger. Her sad eyes meet mine again, then she turns away.

I realise I am too late, just before I begin to fall...

I sat up with a gasp, relieved to discover that I was not plummeting to the ground after all. It had all been a dream. An extraordinarily real dream.

Alpheus's toenails clinked across the barge's floorboards. I twisted around to look for Gabriel.

The curtain to the back cabin pulled back, and he stuck his head in. Seeing me awake, he smiled and pulled the curtain back further. "Hope you slept well, Miss Watson. Tea?"

"Yes, please." I crawled out from under the blankets and got to my knees, squinting towards the window where a hazy beam of sunlight spilled through. "What time is it?"

"It is yet early. The river froze over in the night, but the sun will soon take care of that. We should be on our way by–" He stopped mid-sentence, a look of concern darkening his face. Alpheus had raised his head and was sniffing towards the door. Then he began a low growl, the hackles spiking up on his neck. Next, Billy Bones began to squawk restlessly, "Scurvy dogs! Scurvy dogs!"

Imogen sat up, her eyes wide with terror. The next thing we knew, the barge was shaking from heavy footsteps climbing on board. Someone was pounding on the door and shouting, "Open up in the name of the law!"

What followed was mass confusion. Gabriel limped for the door, but before he could open it to let them in, three policemen with clubs burst through, knocking Gabriel to the floor. One of them pushed him down face forward and began tying his hands behind his back.

Imogen and I were on our feet, both screaming for them to stop, that they were making a mistake; but the other two policemen rushed for us, grabbed us firmly by the shoulders and drove us outside, lifting us and setting us down, still struggling, on the ice-solid ground.

I stopped struggling and froze. Dobbs was standing on the towpath beside Constable Smart. My first feeling was relief to see his familiar face, but then came confusion. *What was Dobbs doing there with the Constable?*

My confusion turned to horror when another figure stepped out from behind the two of them. It was Wix. He wore a wicked, self-satisfied grin and was mumbling away to Constable Smart. "I sees this Nemo fella goin' after these two innocents, an' I says to meself, I says, 'Wix, no good could come o' this.' So I steps in, see, and tries to 'elp the girls only to 'ave my 'ead bashed in by that good-fer-nuffink criminal."

The police appeared actually to be listening to this rubbish, and when Imogen and I tried to protest that it wasn't true, they hushed us up. "Easy now. You've had a shock. You're safe now. There, there." Their mollycoddling was infuriating.

Dobbs rushed forward when he saw us, anxiously asking if we had been hurt. I could hardly hear a word he said, though. My attention kept being drawn away by Wix. He still had the policemen's full attention, and was oozing a lot of hot air.

"I reckon 'e's 'iding more than stolen children in that

barge of 'is. Why, I've often 'eard these bargemen will 'ide fings under the deck boards. I'd check if I was you."

"Go on," the Constable ordered. "Check under the deck."

Gabriel had been dragged out of his barge. He watched the officer take a crowbar and pry up the boards of the boat that was his home. He showed no emotion, just looked on wearily.

"There is something under here, all right," the policeman called out. Next minute, with the help of his fellow officer, he had pulled out a large scrolled-up parchment. The two men unravelled it for all to see.

I felt like an electric shock zapped through my body. It was *The Wedding Feast*. Everyone, including Gabriel, beheld it in shocked silence. Everyone, that is, but Wix.

"See there! Wot did ol' Wix tell yer. Can't trust 'is kind."

"Shut up, you," Constable Smart pushed Wix aside as he came closer to inspect the painting. When he stood up again, he had a look on his face like he'd just won the lottery. "Someone send word to Janklow immediately. And help these young ladies into the carriage before they catch their deaths!"

We were practically hoisted into a carriage. Dobbs and Betsy hopped in after us and the door slammed shut. As the horses started off and we rumbled over the gravel towpath, I turned in my seat. The back window was frosted over, but I could just see the policemen shoving Gabriel into the back of another carriage. It had bars over its windows.

23

JANKLOW & SON

"'Peeping Tom discovered in ladies' swimming bath caught and thrown into pool'... 'More ice accidents for skaters on Thames'... 'Woman gives man sound thrashing at ball for treading on foot and refusing to apologise'... Ah! 'Ere we are." Dobbs flicked the front page of the freshly-printed *Illustrated Police News*. "'Missing painter reappears as notorious St. Paul's thief and kidnapper, see page four.' Let's see if it mentions Bess 'n' me!"

Dobbs had been in a cheery mood ever since our carriage journey the pervious morning. With a brimming smile on his face, he had told us his whole story. He had come to meet us at noon the day before, as planned, and Miss Turvey had given him our message. Instead of waiting around – not being one to waste time – he'd sallied forth to meet us at Regent's Park. He arrived at the Taxopholite Pavilion only just in time to see us scampering off, and then did his best to keep on our trail through the park, across the Euston Road and so on.

"'Tweren't easy neither," he exclaimed. "You must've

taken 'bout fifty detours to get there; 'twas like chasin' after a jack rabbit!"

Dobbs explained how he had learned what had happened to us from his street urchin connections – the rock-throwing boys on the bridge – who had apparently watched the whole violent scene of Wix's attack without bothering to do anything about it. Hearing that Captain Nemo had taken us aboard the *Bella Ramona*, Dobbs naturally assumed, just as we had, that he meant to kidnap us. So, putting old prejudices aside, he had gone straight to Constable Smart for help.

"The ol' Constable didn't believe a word of it at first," Dobbs recounted. "We've not been the best o' friends, him and me. But after I flashed him Inspector Janklow's card 'n' told 'im 'ow I was workin' on the Inspector's orders, he came with me quick 'nough."

And, of course, the rest we knew. Smart found Wix in the wharf. Wix claimed he had played the hero, trying to save us only to be knocked out by the vicious bargeman. And then Wix had uncovered the missing painting on board the *Bella Ramona*, turning him from wanted man to hero with a snap of his dirty fingers.

We had all been taken to the police station for questioning, but every time Imogen and I tried to tell Constable Smart that Wix was lying and that Gabriel had, in fact, rescued us from *him*, his silly little moustache would curl up in a patronising smile.

"There, there, my dears. Con artists like this Gabriel Webb have a great talent for confusing their victims. No doubt, he has persuaded you through trickery that it was he who rescued you from Mr. Wix. Two weak-minded, innocent young ladies are hardly a match for the workings of a criminal mastermind."

When Imogen had retorted that Smart would prove himself to be the one with the weak mind, the Constable had somewhat lost his tender touch. We were in shock, he said, and must be kept under his supervision until Janklow returned and decided what was to be done with us. We were given some food and a room with two camp beds, then left to wait. After an uncomfortable night on a hard cot, a policeman knocked on our door and informed us that Janklow had arrived in the wee hours. He was questioning the prisoner and would meet us for coffee in the station kitchen.

There we waited, listening to Dobbs's happy chatter. After a long time, he noticed how quiet we both were. "I can't 'elp but notice the two o' you look a little bit... cast down considerin' this auspisheeous occasheeon. I reckon it's the shock 'n' all. But never you worry. You was never in any real danger. Not with ol' Dobbs 'n' Janklow on the case!"

At that moment, Inspector Janklow himself appeared in the doorway. The circles under his eyes had darkened several shades, but he greeted us in his usual gentlemanly manner before taking a chair and pouring himself some coffee.

"Well well. There was our culprit, right under our noses all this time."

"What did he say to you?" I asked, eager to find out what Janklow thought, hopeful that he would see what Smart had refused to.

"Nemo has confessed to the identity of Gabriel Webb.

We've caught our man." He smiled weakly. "By we, of course, I mean all of you. And as I understand it, special praise is due to you, Mr. Dobbs, for burying old grudges and alerting the police when you discovered the fate of these two young ladies." He raised his coffee cup in a toast to Dobbs who beamed proudly.

Imogen and I shared a helpless look. What were we to do? Dobbs may have been mistaken about the whole situation, but he *had* acted heroically. Not wanting to steal his moment of glory, I decided the best thing to do was to keep my mouth shut until I could speak to Inspector Janklow privately. I would seize the first opportunity I could find.

The Inspector resumed a business-like air. "I would like to speak to you about the events of the past two days. Gabriel's story does conflict rather with Smart's." He looked from Imogen to me. "But only after you've had time to recover. Smart tells me you've suffered a great shock, and I don't wonder. You've had rather an eventful time of it."

"We're fine, really," I began, but he held up his hand.

"You will accompany me back home. Mrs. Janklow can set you to rights before any questions need be asked."

Neither Imogen nor I argued. Desperate as I was to tell Janklow the truth about what had happened, I was all too happy to leave the constabulary and Constable Smart's smug remarks behind. And anyway, going home with Inspector Janklow offered the best possibility of speaking to him in private.

The four of us, and Betsy, walked together to Bedford Row. When we had reached the Janklow's red door, Dobbs scuffed his shoes on the ground a bit awkwardly. "Well, guess Bess 'n' me'll just be on our way…"

Inspector Janklow frowned. "Whatever do you mean, Mr. Dobbs? You've had as eventful a day as any one of us, and, I might add, proved yourself a fine detective in the making. In fact, I believe a promotion is in order."

Dobbs's eyes grew enormous. "You mean it, gov? Well, wot manner o' promotion did you 'ave in mind?"

Inspector Janklow was giving Dobbs one of his hard but thoughtful stares. "I've been considering branching out from police cases and starting my own private investigations business. Mr. Dobbs, I'd like to train you up proper. You see, you remind me a mite of myself as a boy, full of potential but in bad need of cultivation. If you're to be a decent investigator, you must first be trained up into a decent man."

Dobbs had stars in his eyes. "I can just see it now, gov," he said, raising his hand and swooping it across an imaginary sign in the air in front of him. "Janklow and Dobbs, private investigators."

Inspector Janklow smiled wryly. "I was thinking perhaps… but I'd like your opinion on the matter… of Janklow and Son?"

Dobbs's starry-eyed face became confused. "I didn't know as you had a son, gov…"

"Well," the Inspector looked embarrassed as he turned his hat in his hands. "I suppose I don't as of yet. But I had hoped you might consider taking on that position as well?"

If Dobbs's eyes had been big before, they positively bulged as he digested what the Inspector was saying. His open mouth curled into the biggest, toothiest smile I have ever seen. Then, as suddenly, it dropped. "Inspector, it's not as I don't appreciate the honour of your offer, but…"

"Well, what is it, boy?" Janklow asked with concern.

"Fing is," Dobbs continued, his eyes fixed on Betsy and hers on him, "I could only accept if Bess was welcome to stay with me. And as I know you're not partial to dogs…" He glanced up hopefully, then back down again.

Inspector Janklow eyed the the bulldog thoughtfully. He bent down so that he and the dog were eye to eye, then he spoke directly to her. "You'll have to earn your keep, Bess. Make yourself useful in the kitchen, perhaps."

The bulldog panted for a moment, then shuffled up to the Inspector and gave him an enormous, slobbery lick across the face.

Janklow stood, his face fixed in a tight grimace. "I'm sure Mrs. Janklow will be delighted to have Bess as well."

It was an understatement. When Mrs. Janklow came to the door, her husband presented Dobbs and said, very casually, "Mrs. Janklow, I'm pleased to inform you that Mr. Dobbs has agreed to take the name of Arthur Janklow."

She blinked at her husband, bewildered.

"He has agreed to accept our proposal. Meet your new son, my dear."

"Oh!" Mrs. Janklow wasted no time in throwing herself on Dobbs's neck and crying her eyes out with joy. When she could speak again, she wiped her face and said, "Let's get you cleaned up for dinner, my darling boy. What would you like to eat? Lamb shank? Pot roast? Pork chop? Never you mind, I'll cook up the lot."

24

CAST OFF

*I*t should have been a joyful evening. I was as happy as could be for Dobbs and the Janklows, but I couldn't celebrate. Everything had spun out of order in my head. I had been so sure Gabriel was telling us the truth, yet there was the painting hidden on his barge. Still, whether he had taken the painting or not, I could not believe he was truly a criminal. I felt certain an innocent man had been locked behind bars while the true culprit still walked free.

Imogen felt as gloomy about the whole thing as I did, so we kept to ourselves as much as we could, not wanting to put a damper on the family's happiness.

Mrs. Janklow spent the afternoon cooking up a feast between blowing her nose, wiping her eyes, and beaming at Dobbs as if he were the sun itself and she were basking in its rays.

I hoped I might speak to the Inspector after dinner, but a post boy came to the door with a letter for him and he promptly disappeared with it into his study. To pass the time, we offered to help Mrs. Janklow tidy up, but she insisted we go upstairs and get some rest in the spare bedroom, which was now to be Dobbs's room.

Neither of us had any intention of resting, though. We couldn't have if we wanted to.

"What are you going to tell him?" Imogen asked, sitting cross-legged on the bed with her chin in her hands while I paced back and forth across the tiny room.

"I don't know, exactly. But Gabriel shouldn't be in prison. I'll tell Janklow how it was Wix who attacked us and Gabriel who saved us… and that we know Wix is working for Phineas."

"Are you going to tell him what Gabriel said about Phineas and Ramona disappearing into St. Paul's?"

I thought for a moment. I did not want to tell Janklow anything that sounded too far-fetched, or he would think we were just being fanciful. Yet if it was the truth…

"I'm not sure," I answered. "If only we knew what Phineas was really up to, and could prove it." I rubbed my forehead as if that would spark an idea. "What could he have done with Ramona?"

Imogen bit her thumbnail, thinking. "Gabriel had a point," she said at last. "It wouldn't make sense for Phineas to hurt her if she's the key to his fortune. Besides, what would he paint? She's the subject of every single picture."

I closed my eyes, searching my memory for every detail of the paintings. The Lady of Shalott gazing from her tower window. It had been just like my dream of Ramona and the canary, locked away, as if someone had put them both in a cage.

"I think Phineas is keeping Ramona prisoner in the Middle Ages," I said, and felt sure I'd struck the truth.

Imogen was frowning. "There's just one gaping problem with that," she said. "If Ramona is stuck in the past, how is Phineas travelling back and forth without her? I couldn't have travelled through those paintings if I hadn't been touching you. How is he managing it?"

I dropped down onto the bed beside her and chewed my lip, stumped. I shook my head. "I don't know, but there must be a way. Maybe Gabriel knows something."

"Well good luck getting any information from him. He's in jail for theft and kidnapping, remember?" Imogen let herself fall back onto the bed with a dramatic crash.

I stood up. "That's why we have to speak to Janklow. We have to convince him somehow that Gabriel is innocent."

Imogen shook her head. "Gabriel is right, you know. Janklow is never going to buy the true story."

"Maybe not all of it, but we'll tell him as much as he can handle."

There was a knock at the door.

"Come in!" I called.

It was Dobbs.

"We were just about to come down–" I began, then noticed how tense and red his face was. His ears glowed like hot coals. "What's wrong, Dobbs?"

"The Inspector's 'ad a letter," Dobbs answered without looking me in the eye. "Not sure who from, but he don't seem all too pleased about it. Says he wants to speak to you both straight away."

"We'll be right down," I forced a smile. Why did I feel seasick?

We found Janklow in his study, a piece of paper gripped in his hand. His face appeared more creased and tired than I'd ever seen it.

"Come in," he said in a strangely flat tone.

Imogen and I looked at each other apprehensively but came forward to his desk as he'd asked.

"I believe, Miss Humphreys, that I should pay a visit to your aunt after all that has happened. You have, I hope, informed her that you are safe?"

"I… um…" Imogen gulped. "Yes, I sent her a message yesterday."

"Hmm." Inspector Janklow's nose twitched. "And shall I inform the Misses Turvey as well?"

My heart sank. Janklow offered us the letter he was holding. I took it and, silently, we both began to read.

Dear Sir,

I wish to express my profoundest gratitude to you for recovering what was stolen. That painting remains the greatest work of my life, and posterity is indebted to you for rescuing it from unworthy hands. I say this in writing because, after receiving my knighthood, I will be away seeing to my affairs abroad for some time. You will not hear from me, but whatever reports may arise that I have abandoned my public, pay them no heed. I am merely exerting my talents in some new arena. The artist must follow his muse wherever she takes him, after all.

In my absence, I leave my good name in your trustworthy hands. None better, I am sure.

To that effect, I wish to express something that concerns us both, namely the two young ladies rescued from my poor brother's clutches when the painting was recovered. I was alarmed to learn that these two young ladies were among your informants, for I have reason to suspect that they are more than they pretend to be and may even be employed by my wayward brother (it pains me to say that the lunatic asylum may befit him better than a prison). I have ascertained from Miss Agatha Turvey that they are lodged at her Hostel for Girls of Good Character on Long Acre. I am not sure these girls fit that description.

One could hardly blame even a man of your superior wit if these young ladies have already taken you in, for youthful charms can be so very beguiling. But I issue this word of caution: Do not take them into your confidence. You never know to whom they may be answering. Do not the Scriptures warn us to take care, for one knows not whether he may be entertaining angels? May I humbly posit that, in the case of these two seemingly-innocent girls, one does not know whether he may rather be entertaining demons in angelic disguise.

I trust that you will act in a reasonable manner with this information, for you are, admirably, a man of great Reason.

I remain faithfully,

P.W.W.

Imogen burst as soon as she'd read the letter, "But Inspector, it's all a lie—"

"Is it all a lie, Miss Humphreys?"

"Well... almost all. It is true that we're staying with the Turvey sisters and not with my aunt, but–"

"This is just the trouble," Janklow cut her off without raising his voice. "How am I to trust you as associates if you have been telling me fabrications?"

"Please, Inspector," I was surprised to hear my own voice shaking. "We want to tell you everything. The whole truth. If you'll just let us."

"I should dearly like to hear it, Miss Watson."

"I'm not sure you will like it, though. It's a little... hard to believe."

Janklow frowned. "Miss Watson, the truth is always reasonable."

I did my best to steady my breathing. Then I told him, starting with all that had happened the previous day, and how Gabriel had really rescued us from Wix. I told him Gabriel's story, what he had seen at St. Paul's. And then I even dared to tell him what Gabriel believed to be the explanation for Ramona's disappearance. "We think he's right, because..." Janklow had listened impassively to my entire explanation, but I still had trouble voicing the words, "because Imogen and I... we came to 1885 the very same way. Through a painting. In fact, through the very painting that appeared there that night. That's why we were running from St. Paul's after the Mass on Christmas Eve. The painting brought us there, right to the scene of the crime. And then we met you, and... well, you know the rest."

When I had finished, he just looked at me. Only then did I notice some sort of emotion in his eyes. It wasn't anger. It was as if a battle were going on inside his own head, though I could only see faint flickers of it from the outside. Finally, he let his eyes drop to his desk.

"I must confess, Miss Watson, that I have never been more… disappointed."

I felt like I'd just received a punch to the stomach, and there was more to come.

"You might at least do me the courtesy of being honest now. But I blame myself." He pointed one of his long fingers at his own chest. "I, a grown man and professional detective, should never have involved children in such matters. I do not believe you to be, as the letter suggests, demons in disguise. Misguided, perhaps. And as I have no evidence that you conspired with Gabriel Webb in his theft–"

"But Inspector, please–"

"Let me finish, Miss Watson. As there is no evidence of conspiracy, I will not press charges *this* time. But from this moment, every connection between us must be severed forever. And I plead with you to sever all connections with that imprisoned man, for next time, I will not be able to look the other way. There shall be serious consequences."

For the first time that day, I really did feel in shock. "Inspector," I pleaded, "Won't you at least look at the evidence for our side of the story? What if we really are telling you the truth?"

"No matter how much I wish to believe you, Reason forbids me."

I slammed my hand down on his desk. "But what if the most rational explanation *is* magic?"

A moment of silence followed. My hand tingled. He looked at it a moment. Then, as if wanting distraction, somewhere to look besides at Imogen and me, he took out his pocketwatch and held it between both hands. "You'll never be a detective, Miss Watson," he said, fumbling the watch open. "A detective needs cold, clear-headed Reason. Not fairy stories. That stuff is for the nursery, not the constabulary. Now I must ask you to collect your things and leave my home at once. I'll make up some excuse to tell Mrs. Janklow and Arthur. The truth would only upset them."

I didn't budge. Hot tears stung my eyes, but I couldn't even brush them away. Then Imogen took hold of my arm and pulled me away from the office. The Inspector never looked up. His eyes stayed glued to his pocketwatch as if hoping to find the truth on its cold face.

25

NO TIME FOR TEARS

"Katie, slow down! Do you even know where you're going?"

I flung myself through the iron gates of Lincoln's Inn Fields. No, I didn't know where I was going, but I couldn't stop and wait for Imogen to catch up to me. I was too ashamed for her to see the tears pouring uncontrollably down my cheeks.

Shame was all I knew in that moment. It felt as heavy as wet concrete being poured over my shoulders until I could hardly breathe. Unable to take another step for the weight of it, I collapsed, a miserable heap, onto the nearest bench.

Imogen caught up and dropped down beside me. I covered my face with my hands, but I couldn't hold back the choking sobs that gave me away. I had been in some terrible fixes before and still managed to keep from crying. But the memory of Janklow's face – that look of disappointment – and his parting words, "You'll never be a detective, Miss Watson"… The sting of those words was worse than any cut or bruise I'd suffered. It was more than I could bear.

Imogen didn't speak at first. She waited until my sobs died down into sniffles, then handed me her frilly handkerchief to wipe my running nose.

"It's not fair, what Janklow said." She didn't sound upset. Just matter-of-fact. "But none of it was true, you know? You really shouldn't take it so much to heart, Katie."

I knew she was trying to help; but instead of feeling better, I felt a flare of anger and looked away. How could Imogen talk so calmly, as if it didn't matter what Janklow thought of me? This had been my chance to prove that I had what it took to be a real detective, that I wasn't just some kid playing games. Now, he thought of me not only as a silly kid, but a lying one.

"You don't understand," I muttered, my watery eyes fixed on the ground. "Without Janklow, it's hopeless."

"What do you mean, hopeless?" Imogen's voice was laced with her old sarcasm. "You've managed just fine without Janklow before now. Why is he suddenly so important?" She sounded impatient, annoyed. It made my anger flare up all the more.

"Because he's a real detective!" I shouted. "He knows what he's doing. And I … I don't. What he said might've been based on lies, but he was right about one thing. I'll never be a good detective. I can't do this. It's too big for me. I give up."

After a long, self-loathing pause, Imogen finally answered, her voice quiet but sharp. "So that's it? You're just giving up because one person doesn't think you're amazing? What about Ramona? What about your promise to Jim and Ka-Ti... and getting home to our families? None of that matters now because of one person's *wrong* opinion of you?"

I blinked at her, stunned. I thought she would leave me to wallow in my misery, not tell me to buck up and get over myself. It hadn't occurred to me how selfish I was being. My decision to give up didn't just affect me. It meant giving up on her and everyone else too.

"You know, Katie," – she still had a piece of her mind to give me – "I was so desperate to come with you on this adventure because ... because I believed in you. Back in Cherokee Country, you never gave up on me. Even when I was horrible to you, you still fought against all the odds and came after me. I thought I could count on you to see this thing through, but I guess I was wrong."

Imogen's words cut way deeper than Janklow's; they struck true as an arrow striking a bullseye. I felt my eyes stinging again as she stood up and stormed down the pathway. But this time, I fought back the tears. This was not a time for wallowing. I knew now that this, of all times, was a time for taking action.

"Wait, Im." I sprinted after her.

She spun around, arms crossed over her chest.

I sniffled and looked her square in the eye. "We will find Ramona, and we will get home again. I'm not giving up. Not yet. Not as long as you'll stick this out with me."

Her iron glare softened, and she gave me one of her signature eye rolls. "Honestly, Katie. You know I'm not going anywhere. *Obviously.*"

The best way I knew how to thank her for pulling me

out of the pit of despair was to throw my arms around her neck.

She hugged me back, all the while grumbling in my ear, "Ok. Ok. Are we going to solve this thing now or wait 'til next Christmas?"

We found another bench, and I pulled out my pen and notebook with a vengeance, like a knight unsheathing my sword for combat. "Right. Let's go over the facts again. If our theory is correct, Phineas had Wix hide the painting on Gabriel's barge. The question is, why?"

"Well that's obvious, isn't it?" Imogen answered. "He did it to get Gabriel arrested, to make sure he didn't get in the way."

"Yes, but in the way of what?"

"Whatever it is he's planning."

I rubbed my hands together to warm them, then picked up the notebook. "It's strange, isn't it?" I flipped through the pages right to the back and took the picture of the Webb brothers from its pocket. "They look so close. I bet they never thought then they'd wind up enemies."

"Katie, did you write that?" Imogen was craning her neck to peer at the notebook lying open in my lap. "That handwriting looks an awful lot like–"

My eyes dropped to the page. "Phineas Webb's," I breathed, snatching up the book and holding it close to my face. How hadn't I noticed the note scribbled onto the back page … a note in loopy, cursive writing, identical to the writing that had churned my stomach just an hour earlier.

My mind was in a flurry as I read out the message, growing angrier with each word:

My Dears,

I write to advise you: keep your distance from my brother or I shall have no choice but to discredit you as well as him. I truly thought Gabriel could sink no lower, but he has proved me wrong by employing children to spy for him. I have known you were acting as his agents since your visit to Camelot. This notebook, which my manservant confiscated, only confirmed my suspicions. Your uncanny interest in my model and your eagerness to examine my pocketwatch told me at once that Gabriel had sent you. I do not doubt he is most sore about losing his beloved trinket. But in truth, I feel no remorse for asking Wix to take it. The watch was wasted on Gabriel, a mere sentimental plaything, like Ramona herself. I alone saw what a rare and valuable treasure that little bird was, the worlds it could open.

I tell you this so that you may pass it on to my dear brother when I am gone. He should not look for me, for where I go, he cannot follow. I must now embrace my Destiny, as he must be embraced by his. Tell him this, then you will do well never to speak to him again. I fear his reputation shall only sink lower after I depart. I should be sorry to see two young ladies in the bloom of their youth pulled down into the mire alongside him.

I bear you no ill will, but bid you farewell as a friend,
P.W.W.

"A *friend*? Is he serious?" Imogen made a snarling noise. Her fists were clenched and she looked ready to pummel the first person to cross her path. "What's with all these notes, anyway? Doesn't he have the guts to say what he wants to say to our faces?" I still stared at the letter, my eyes retracing the line about the pocketwatch being wasted on Gabriel... about its ability to open worlds...

Like a hammer striking a bell, the answer to a long-muddled-over riddle rang loud and clear in my mind until it burst from my mouth: "He's been using the pocketwatch to get through the painting!"

Imogen stopped ranting and looked at me dumbfounded.

"The canary sings Ramona's grandmother's song," I explained. "That's how he's been bringing the painting to life without her!" My palm flew up to meet my forehead. "How did I not see it sooner?"

Imogen was still staring at me with her mouth wide open. She seemed to be hatching a thought. At last she said, "It still doesn't add up, though."

I waited for her to explain.

"I mean, it would all make sense if Phineas still had the painting. He uses the watch, plays the song, slips through the painting, *voilà*! But he doesn't have it. The police do. And he's the one who made sure they'd find it... that is, *if* we're right and Wix really did plant it on the barge."

I bit my lip, thinking hard. She was right; it didn't add up. If Phineas was planning a getaway, he would need the painting. I bit so hard I tasted blood on my lip.

"What if we've been wrong the whole time?" Imogen muttered. "What if Gabriel really did steal the painting to protect Ramona?"

I shook my head, but the tiniest seed of doubt was beginning to bud. *What if he did? Or what if the painting had nothing to do with Phineas's plan?* The doubts were like tiny holes in a boat, letting despair seep in and flood my mind.

Action. I needed to take action before I drowned in questions.

"We need to speak to Gabriel," I said. "We're missing something. Maybe there's another painting or... oh I don't know. But if anyone can help us figure out what Phineas is up to, it's him."

Imogen looked at me doubtfully. "Sure. But there's just this teensy little problem. Gabriel is locked away in a jail cell, remember?"

The sound of quick steps crunching the frosty walkway and heavy, gurgled breaths made me twist around in my seat. Dobbs was running up the path towards us; the gurgling was Betsy at his heels. I was so happy to see him, I sprang to my feet. His wide, toothy grin lit up his whole face when he spotted us.

"Law," he panted, his breath coming out in puffs. "Bess 'n' me've been searchin' for the two of ya high 'n' low!"

"Does Inspector Janklow know you've come looking for us?" I asked, wondering how much Dobbs knew about the letter and what had passed between us and the Inspector.

"Think so," he said, straightening up. "'E was the one wot told me I was to make sure you made it safely back to the Misses Turveys'."

"He did?" I couldn't believe it. Janklow didn't despise us? He still cared whether we were safe or not?

Dobbs nodded. "Wouldn't tell me why you left, though. Just said the case of the missin' paintin' was closed 'n' we weren't to be seein' one another anymore." A hurt expression came over Dobbs's face. "But that don't explain why you 'ad to go without so much as a 'by your leave'. I was beginnin' to think you didn't care whether we met again... That is..." His ears sticking out from beneath his hat rim shone bright red. "Wot I meant was, Bess didn't much like bein' dropped so sudden-like. She 'as a very sensitive 'art, ya know."

I bent down to rub Bessy's wrinkly head. "We *do* care, Bessy," I told the dog, making sure Dobbs could hear me loud and clear. "You're a true friend. We could never drop you."

I looked up and locked eyes with Dobbs. He beamed at me, then looked quickly down at his feet. Toeing the frosty ground, he said, "So I reckon you'll not be needin' a chaperone anymore, now the case is closed 'n' all."

"Actually, Dobbs, we do need your help." I glanced at Imogen and she gave me an approving nod. "Janklow was mistaken. The case of the missing painting is still very much open."

He cocked his head. "Janklow mistaken?"

"It's not his fault," I answered quickly. "He's been hoodwinked. We wish we could explain everything, but there's not time. Phineas Webb is plotting something. We believe he planted that painting on Gabriel's barge to get him out of the way. He set the whole thing up so that Janklow wouldn't believe Gabriel... or us."

Dobbs sank onto the bench looking stricken. "You mean to say Gabriel Webb's an innocent man 'n' I called the coppers on 'im?"

"You did the right thing, Dobbs," I assured him. "You were just looking out for us, just like you were supposed to." I looked at Imogen who nodded in agreement.

"Yea," she added, "It's Phineas who's caused all this to happen. Not you."

"Which is why we have to stop him," I said. "But we need your help. We need to speak to Gabriel."

Dobbs scratched Bessy's head, thinking and chewing on his lip. Finally, he sat up. "Miss Katie. You know I'd 'elp you if I could, but 'ow am I s'posed to get you past the Constable wot's guarding the Cap'n?"

I laid my hand on his shoulder. "You're Arty Dobbs," I said. "If anyone could think of a way to slip past the bobbies unnoticed, it's you."

He puffed up proudly, but deflated the next second, shaking his head. "Sorry, Miss Katie. Miss Imogen. I'd like to 'elp ya, but I'm 'fraid I can't 'ave no part in it."

I felt a fresh stab of shame. "What do you mean, Dobbs?"

"I've turned over a new leaf, 'member? I'm a partner in Janklow and Son now. And besides, what would me new Ma think of me? I am sorry," his head hung, wagging back and forth. "If it was anyfink else, I'd be at your service, but I've given all that up. I'm for the law now. And I'd advise you two not to go crossin' it."

Imogen looked as though she'd just been slapped. I'm sure neither of us ever thought we'd be getting a lecture from Arty Dobbs about crossing the law. But one look at him told me how much he was struggling himself. Despite feeling hurt, I was proud of him.

"You're right, Dobbs. We won't ask you to cross the law. But Imogen and I have to do this. We have to stop Phineas because ... well, because it's the right thing to do. You don't have to be involved. You can forget we ever had this conversation. Just, please, don't tell Janklow. We'll figure the rest out on our own."

Dobbs tensed and screwed his eyes shut, as if squeezing every muscle of willpower, then, all in a rush, he let it go with a sigh. "No offence, misses, but you've got 'bout as much chance of findin' an ha'penny in an haystack as getting' past that Constable without Bess 'n' me to 'elp ya."

26

MONKEY TRIBE OF THE METROPOLIS

*D*obbs staged a plan within the hour. After a quick round-up, he managed to rally a handful of his fellow street Arabs to come to our aid. We met them in a back alley near Covent Garden Market. There was Willie the Slink, the tall, dirty boy Dobbs had greeted in the market days before; a squat, square little boy called Gus who wore his flat cap down over his eyes; and two scrappy-looking, white-blonde-headed girls, Sally and Tilda, who introduced themselves as the Mudlark Twins.

The Arabs listened with the sombre respect of soldiers to their general as Dobbs gave them their orders. Willie the Slink, who was already a familiar face to the local constabulary, was to act suspiciously to draw the Constable out onto the street, then give him the slip. Sally would play the part of snitch, telling the Constable what she had witnessed of Willie's made-up crimes and which way she thought she'd seen him take off. Meanwhile, Tilda would help herself to his keys. Apparently, the twins were famous for this double-act pick-pocketing tactic.

I felt a little squeamish about the plan by the time we got in position around the corner from the police station, but the gang of Arabs looked as cool as cucumbers.

Dobbs was giving his last briefings as the bells tolled half past nine. "Remember, Gus, you're on watch. Two rooster crows as soon as you catch sight o' Constable Smart headin' back to the station. I want sharp eyes out, got it?"

Gus saluted, his eyes still invisible beneath his hat. I privately wondered how good a watch he would prove to be.

Dobbs peered around the corner to take stock. "Well, this is it," he said.

"Dobbs." I was getting cold feet. "What if Constable Smart catches Willie before Sally has the chance to stop him?"

Dobbs and the others all snickered. "Why, Miss Katie, you'd make a stuffed bird laugh," Dobbs said, bracing his belly. "Smart's no match for Willie the Slink. I'll be painted pink if Willie don't manage to slip through his daddles."

Imogen looked at me as if to see whether I had understood a single word. I shook my head and decided not to ask any more questions.

Dobbs resumed his watch, waiting for the right moment, then turned to Willie and gave the signal, raising an invisible pistol and pulling the trigger. Willie dashed out from hiding, one hand hidden beneath his coat flap, looking this way and that and slinking – I could see why he'd been given his name – past the police station in a convincingly guilty manner.

It was only seconds before we heard Smart. "Oi, you! Not another step! I said... ah, dash him."

The Mudlark twins slipped out next. The plan was in motion.

"Follow me!" Dobbs whispered hoarsely. We tiptoed around the corner and ducked into the station, Gus taking his position right outside the door.

Dobbs led us through the front room to a big, black iron door with a padlock. He turned back towards the door to the street just in time to see Tilda appear and toss a ring of keys. Dobbs snatched it out of the air, fumbled for a key, and opened the padlock in a wink. Behind the door was a dark, arched brick hallway with two iron doors on either side.

Dobbs cupped his mouth. "Psst! Nemo!" the whisper echoed and came back. A narrow window slid open in the second door to our left. Dobbs stayed at the hallway's entrance while Imogen and I ran to the open window. A pair of grey eyes peered out at us.

"What are you two doing here? Does Janklow know?" Gabriel's voice was soft but firm.

"No," I answered truthfully.

"Then you shouldn't be here." He began to slide the window shut.

"Wait! Mr. Webb, please. There's not time to explain, but we *have* to speak to you. We need your help if we're going to rescue Ramona."

The window slid slowly open again. "Rescue her? Have you found out where she is?"

"We have an idea, but first we need to know... the

painting found on your boat. Did you...?" I cut short. Gabriel was giving me a strange, searching look.

"You know," he said. "There is something of her in you. Something in the eyes." He seemed to be wrestling with himself. "You really are determined to find her, aren't you?"

I nodded.

He nodded back. "All that I told you was the truth, Miss Watson. I did not steal it. I was framed." He gave a short, dry laugh. "A painter framed for stealing a painting. Sounds like a lame joke, does it not?"

"We didn't think you did it," I said hastily. "But there's still one thing we can't work out. If the painting is so important to Phineas, why would he steal it just to frame you with it? Especially if *The Wedding Feast* really is his doorway to the past... why would he let it go?"

"Ah." I could tell from the creases in the corner of his eyes he was smiling. "You're asking the right questions, Miss Watson. Go on. You're a clever one. I'll bet you can work it out."

I wasn't sure that I could, but I closed my eyes, thinking back over all that I knew of Phineas Webb ... our meeting with him... his paintings... his strange behaviour when Imogen uncovered the canvas... I opened my eyes, the answer on my tongue. "Because it's a fake. The painting on your barge was a fake. We saw it in his house."

Imogen gasped. "Oh my goodness, of course! That's why he was so upset when I uncovered it! He was only just getting started, but it looked just like *The Wedding Feast*."

Gabriel was smiling grimly. "Bravo," he said. "You really are good little detectives. Janklow should be proud to have you by his side."

I swallowed, not wanting to admit the truth about what Janklow thought of us. "But if the police have the fake painting," I said, quickly returning to task, "then where is the real one?"

"Wherever Phineas intends to use it. Somewhere he deems important and sufficiently secret."

"We think we've worked out how he's been travelling through it without Ramona's help." I said, holding the notebook up to the window open to Phineas's note.

Gabriel squinted to read it in the dim light, his eyes growing stormier with each line. "It is just as I feared," he said. "He intends to make a grand exit, and he has the means to do it. His plan has succeeded at every point. All his life, my brother has wanted nothing more than to rule as the lord over some medieval castle. He fancies himself quite the knight in shining armour."

Imogen gave a disdainful snort. "He already has Camelot, not to mention fame and fortune."

"Oh no, Miss Humphreys. Phineas could never be satisfied with make believe; not if he can have the real thing. Now that he has his precious knighthood, there is nothing holding him back from making his dreams a reality."

Panic gripped me like icy fingers. "But then there's not time!" I blurted. "He said in his note to Janklow he was leaving after his knighthood ceremony. If he leaves tonight, that's it. Ramona–"

"Ramona will be out of our reach forever," Gabriel finished solemnly.

I felt frantic. "We have to stop him. We have to go." I paused long enough to look into Gabriel's stormy eyes. "But what about you? We can't just leave you in here."

"Forget about me, Miss Watson. I am of no consequence. But listen to me, both of you. You cannot face my brother alone. Phineas is–"

But at that very second, two rooster crows sounded from outside. Dobbs came flying into the dark corridor. "Gus was slow on the uptake. Smart's already at the door! We gotta back slang it!"

Imogen looked at him blankly. "Uh, sorry?"

Dobbs waved his hands wildly towards the back of the corridor. "Go out the back!" He fumbled with the key ring, trying two of the keys in the bolt with no luck.

"What's goin' on in 'ere?" Smart roared from the front room.

"Come on, come on, come on!" Imogen whispered through gritted teeth.

Dobbs tried a third key, and it slid into the lock. He unbolted the door and swung it open just as heavy footsteps boomed in the corridor behind us.

"Oi, you three! Stand still!"

We hurled ourselves out the door into a dingy, stone courtyard locked in by tall brick walls. Dobbs waved us over to the wall and made a cradle with his hands. "Go on!"

He gave Imogen, then me a leg up so we were able to heave ourselves over the wall and drop down to the other side. I heard him grunt as he hoisted himself up after us.

His top half was just visible over the wall when he slid back.

"I've got ya! You're not gettin' away this time!" Smart's muffled, jubilant shouts came from the other side. Dobbs's head was bobbing up and down as he tried to keep his grip. Smart must have caught him by the foot. We were helpless to do anything; Dobbs was too high up on the wall for us to reach his hands and pull him over to safety.

Smart shouted again, more violently than ever. "You don't stop puttin' up a fight, I'll 'ave your dog minced up for sausages!"

Dobbs made a face like he'd just been punched as he swung a look over his shoulder down at Betsy. In our flight, we'd all forgotten she was still behind, in the station yard.

"Don't worry, Bess, I'll not abandon ye!" He called down. "I give in, Constable. Let go of me leg 'n' I'll come down."

"No tricks!" the Constable snarled.

"No tricks," Dobbs agreed lifelessly over his shoulder. He turned back to us with sorrowful eyes. "Tell the Janklows I'm sorry I let 'em down. Now get goin' 'n' find that lady." With that, his fingers loosened and he disappeared behind the wall.

27

DESPERATE MEASURES

"Now where are we going? Katie, stop!"

I stopped at the top of Bedford Row just long enough to explain myself. "We have to tell Janklow. We have to get Dobbs out of there."

"Katie, you can't–"

"I have to, Im. He shouldn't be in there. This is all my fault." I marched towards the Janklows' red door, ready to pound it with my fist until I got an answer. Whatever followed, I was ready to face it.

But before I could step up to the door to knock, Imogen threw herself between me and it. "Katie, listen to me. I mean it."

Her face was as serious as a heart attack, and I found myself taking a step back. "Imogen, please move."

"Weren't you listening? Janklow said if we ever had anything to do with Gabriel Webb again, there would be consequences. If you tell him we've just broken into prison to speak to Gabriel, there's no chance he'll simply let us go on our merry way. We'll end up in one of those cells too."

"I have to at least try to explain to Janklow," I pleaded. "I can't just leave him–"

"You can't save everyone! You have to choose. It's Dobbs or Ramona. And bear in mind, without Ramona, we may never get back home again."

I stood paralysed. Inside, the feeling of being torn in two was so terrible, it made me want to scream. How could I choose?

"I'll deal with Janklow. You should go, before it's too late."

I looked at Imogen, confused. "What? You mean split up?"

"You can't do both, so leave Dobbs to me."

"But I can't face Phineas without you," I protested.

"Yes you can. You'll find a way to stop him. If anyone can do it, Katie, it's you. You were meant to find Ramona, remember?"

With those words, my dream flashed before my mind… the hopelessness in Ramona's eyes. With a deep breath, I reached out and met Imogen in a tight embrace. "How will we find each other? We need a meeting place."

She thought a second. "At St. Paul's. Where this all began."

I nodded, still holding her hand. I didn't want to leave her, to think of the possibility that we might never find each other again.

Gently, she pulled her hand away from mine. "Go, Katie."

I knew the time for hesitation was over. Without another word, I turned and ran down Bedford Square, the distant bell chiming along with the thuds of my footsteps.

I SKIDDED to a halt under the shadows of Covent Garden Market and looked up at the clock face on the church steeple. Eleven o'clock. One more hour and the night would be over. Even if I ran the whole distance, I would never get to Camelot in time. What if I was already too late?

No. I must not think like that. There must be a way to–

My thoughts were interrupted by a cacophony of honking and braying. My heart gave a leap. *Samson!*

With the help of my penlight, I raced through the market's dark passageways, out the other side of the pavilion and up to the dilapidated little shed that housed the one-eyed mule. "Oh Samson, I am *so* glad to see you," I panted, slinging open the shed door and giving him my hand to smell. He nibbled at my sleeve.

"I'm sorry, I don't have any apples today. But if you get me to Bloomsbury, I promise you a treat."

He nodded his big, clumsy head, appeased. Trying not to startle him in my frenzy, I snatched the halter off a nail in the wall and slipped it over his nose and stiff ears. I found a rope coiled up on the ground and made makeshift reins out of it. Then, with the help of an upturned feed bucket, I hoisted myself over Samson's broad back and braced myself for the kick-up.

He didn't move a muscle.

"Samson, *ya!*" I urged him forward with all my might. Still nothing.

If only I had inherited Ka-Ti's horse whispering skills. My mind was racing for a way to get the mule moving when I nearly jumped out of my skin. That crazy rooster had stuck his head up out of the hay. He must've thought my flashlight was the morning sun, because he was crowing his head off. But that crow had the effect of a shotgun. Samson bucked his hind legs and took off before I could find my balance.

I managed to stay on him and steer him to the left, just in time before he ran into the glass windows of a market shop. After a bit of bouncing and swaying side to side, I managed to wrangle him under control. He seemed thrilled to be out of his shed with free run of the streets. I tried him a little faster. He picked up pace like an Ascot race horse, and we were flying over the cobblestones of Long Acre in no time.

As we passed the Misses Turveys' Hostel for Girls of Good Character, I couldn't help imagining the look on Agatha Turvey's face were she to gaze out the window at that moment and see me riding bareback on a mule through the London streets.

When we reached the wide thoroughfare of Kingsway, I pulled Samson to a halt. Raucous crowds celebrating the New Year poured out of taverns and mingled in the street. Cab drivers swerved and called out angry threats. It was mayhem.

My heart dropped. I had not counted on this delay.

"Turn around, Samson. We'll have to find another way."

But the mule, bewitched by his newfound freedom, had no intention of turning around. Rather, he lowered his head and bolted straight down the middle of the road. There was nothing I could do but get low and hold on for my life as people in fancy dress leapt out of the way while others catcalled and cheered us on.

I was breathless and shaking by the time we reached the quiet of Bloomsbury Square Gardens, thankfully without a single collision despite Samson's having only one eye. He slowed to a trot as another bell somewhere nearby struck once – eleven thirty – and I knew I had the mule to thank for getting me to Bloomsbury before midnight.

"Well done, boy," I whispered as I slipped off his back and led him under the big chestnut tree in the garden square.

Samson didn't waste any time but set straight to chomping frosted chestnuts. "There you go. I promised you a reward, didn't I?" I said, patting his neck, my hand still shaking.

A soft murmur of voices caught my attention. I looked for the sound. It seemed to be coming from across the street, in the high hedges surrounding Camelot. I dropped down out of sight and listened, not daring to blink or to breathe.

There was just enough lamplight to see a turbaned figure appear at the house's grand gate. The turban turned one way, then the other, as if expecting someone's arrival.

Who he was expecting became clear the next second with the sound of elegantly clopping hooves followed by the appearance of Phineas Webb's four magnificent white horses drawing his carriage.

My eyes were as wide as a watchful owl's. *Could Phineas be inside the carriage? Might he only now be returning with his knighthood to make his grand exit? Maybe I wasn't too late after all ... but how was I to stop him now?*

The horses came to a halt in front of the gate, the leader stomping his front hoof with a mighty snort. Behind me, Samson raised his head suddenly. Becoming aware of the horses, he let out a screeching bray, like a door swinging on rusty hinges. My hair stood up on end as the horses responded with disgruntled whinnies. Then the turbaned man called out, "Who is there? Show yourself."

Terrified beyond thinking, I crawled on my belly through the crunchy, frosted grass and rolled beneath the bench, pulling my skirt hem under just in time before the light of his lantern swept the ground. It paused when it found Samson. I squeezed my eyes tightly shut and held my breath.

"What is it?" A second voice called; I guessed it was the carriage driver's.

"It is only a blind mule." The turbaned man sounded irritated to have been drawn across the street for such a pathetic spectacle.

"What is the meaning of this?"

I clasped my hand over my mouth. It was Phineas who spoke.

"Sir, it is nothing." The turbaned man's lantern beam turned and retreated hastily back to the gate. I squirmed to the end of the bench and peered out. I could just see a tall top hat waiting at the gate. The turbaned man dashed over to it, bowed, then opened the door of the carriage.

So Phineas wasn't coming. He was going!

The tall, top-hatted figure climbed into the carriage.

The door shut, and the manservant nodded to the driver who in turned cracked a whip at the four white horses.

He was getting away! I scrambled to my feet, peeling the wet skirt from my legs. I took one look at Samson. I needed to follow Phineas without being apprehended. The mule had proved himself a fast mode of transport, but certainly not a stealthy one.

The carriage reached the corner, about to turn out of the square, when I had a sudden inspiration.

My hands half frozen from lying on the ground, I fumbled with Samson's ropes and secured them to the bench. Then I turned and ran as fast as my wet skirt would allow. The carriage had stopped to let a cab pass. I had nearly caught up with it when the driver once again cracked his whip. I didn't slow down, but thrust out my hand and grabbed hold of one of the big back wheels, just as I'd seen Dobbs do, at the same time launching myself off the ground. My foot landed firmly on the back step, and I grabbed hold of a lantern hanger over my head as the carriage lurched around the corner.

I felt a moment's elation and wished Dobbs had been there to see me. But as the carriage rattled on down dark, deserted streets, a sense of cold dread crept into my bones. I was in deep now. Whatever destiny Phineas was riding towards, when we got there, I would have to face him alone.

28

DOOM IN THE DOME

A fiercely cold wind whipped up as the carriage rattled down Fleet Street, past the Royal Courts and the guarding dragon; past Ye Olde Cheddar Cheese, its misted windows glimmering with lights and silhouettes of folk celebrating the New Year inside. It was déjà vu, making the same journey Imogen and I had made our first night in 1885, only in reverse. I knew even before I saw the dome rising up against the cloud-shrouded sky that this journey would end where it all began: St. Paul's Cathedral.

The white horses pranced around the side of the cathedral until the driver called *"Whoa!"* and pulled them to a stop in an adjacent courtyard. There was not a single streetlamp to be seen; all I could see were shadows moving about the carriage.

I couldn't move. My fingers still clung to the lantern hanger, stiff and stinging from the icy wind. My eyes watered, but I forced them to stay open, watching for movement in the darkness.

The carriage door opened. Phineas was getting out; I could just make out the rim of his top hat against the shadows. His footsteps and cane rapped against the cobblestones. He was walking towards the cathedral.

Without warning, the carriage began to move off. I wrenched open my aching fingers and leapt, landing crookedly on the cobbles and falling onto my hip. I bit my tongue, but a grunt still managed to escape me.

The footsteps and cane stopped, then came closer. Softly as I could, I scrambled towards the wall of the cathedral and ducked behind a holly hedge. The prickly leaves stuck through my dress and pricked my skin, but I didn't move.

From this angle, I could make out Phineas's silhouette. It stopped and turned, as if looking for what had made the noise. At last, he cleared his throat and his steps resumed their purposeful patter towards the cathedral.

He stopped in the graveyard. I was sure he was standing over the very big stone tomb with the sleeping knight carved on it that Imogen and I had hidden behind that first night, when Constable Smart had pursued us. I never would have guessed then that in a few short nights, I'd be the one doing the pursuing through that very graveyard. And I certainly never could have guessed what would happen next.

I heard a scraping sound of rock against rock. Phineas must have pushed the lid bearing the sleeping knight right off the coffin's base, because the next thing I saw was a ghostly hand holding a lantern rising up from the tomb. It hovered in front of Phineas Webb, as if floating in mid-air.

Just when I thought things could get no creepier,

Phineas swung one leg over the side of the open coffin, then the other. Next thing I knew, he disappeared. I could hear the scraping noise of the lid being closed again from the inside.

As soon as the sound stopped, I sprang from my hiding place and pointed my penlight at the stone knight. He looked undisturbed, but as I swept the light over the coffin's side, I discovered the big slab of stone had not been sealed back properly. The lid sat slightly ajar, leaving a crack big enough for my fingers to slide into.

It took every ounce of my strength to move that stone, but just when I thought I couldn't push any harder, it gave. The lid slid away, leaving the tomb gaping open.

Shaking, I held my penlight over the black opening. My mouth dropped open. It was not a tomb at all, but a trap door! I was looking down a flight of rough stone stairs.

I sat on the tomb's edge and threw my legs over. I allowed myself just one deep breath before descending into the earth's cold, dark belly.

The stairs dead-ended into a suffocatingly narrow passageway haunted by the sounds of drippy pipes and scurrying rodents. One day, I would thank Charlie for the gift of that penlight. Its faithful little beam was the only thing that kept me going. I fixed my eyes on the spot of light in front of me, thinking only of my next step and refusing to imagine what might be lurking in the darkness all around me.

One step at a time, I coached myself. I could feel the floor slanting gradually upwards. Every few paces, I paused to listen out for Phineas up ahead, but he was too far ahead of me to hear.

One riddle at least was solved: I now knew how Phineas had been getting in and out of the cathedral undetected; but I could not imagine how he could have removed an enormous painting like *The Wedding Feast* through that passage when I could hardly move through it without bumping up against its wet walls.

The fear that Phineas had turned into some secret side tunnel was beginning to grip me when the passageway ended, opening up into a larger chamber. I must have been within the cathedral walls, but where, I could hardly guess. I paused. Footsteps echoed distantly somewhere above. My eyes rose up and up and up, and it began to dawn on me just how immense a chamber I was in. At a dizzying height, the lantern – along with whoever carried it – was making its way up an open, spiralling ladder.

I dropped my eyes and shuffled across the floor until my toe nudged the base of the ladder. Clicking off my penlight, I gripped the cold, iron rail and started to climb.

What felt like an eternity of steps later, I stepped up onto another platform. I was broken out in a cold sweat, every limb shaking uncontrollably. Knowing one false step would send me plummeting into the dark abyss below, I held out my hands and shuffled forward. My hands touched the frame of a doorway. I slid my fingers down until they locked around a doorknob.

I turned the knob and pushed. It didn't budge. I leaned into the door with my shoulder and felt a resistance from the other side, as if someone was holding the door closed. I rammed it with the whole side of my body.

This time, the door opened and I gasped at the shock of freezing wind and needle-sharp sleet. The wind whipped up my hair and skirt as I tried to step out onto an outer walkway. I turned my face away from the wind and only then realised where I was. I had climbed all the way to the cathedral dome. I was standing just outside its base with only a stone railing between me and the world below.

Shielding my eyes from the sleet, I edged into the wind and peered through the rails. Down below, London looked like a toy city, its streetlamps just pinpricks of light in a sea of sooty blackness.

I stepped back, bracing myself against the side of the dome. The thought of meeting Phineas out there chilled me more than the wind. I had to find him before he found me. But which way would he have gone?

A loud banging sound above sent my heart leaping into my throat. I craned back my head and saw an open door. The wind was flapping it about on its hinges. A narrow staircase wrapped around the outer dome leading up to the door, nearly to the very top. I remembered Imogen telling me about the Golden Gallery… how just looking up at it from the cathedral floor had given me butterflies.

But apart from the earth below, it was the only place Phineas could have gone from where I stood. I could not turn back now.

The wind fought with my skirt as I climbed the stairs, but at least it pressed me against the wall as there was nothing much to hold on to. As I scaled the final steps approaching the door, sudden dread gripped my chest. I did not want to walk through that door, but I couldn't go back either.

What was I doing here? How I wished to goodness I had a plan… a weapon… just someone there beside me.

I closed my eyes as another gust of wind swelled up with a loud hum.

No. It wasn't humming… It was singing… It was Ramona's song, clear as anything! But it couldn't be the wind. It was coming from inside!

Just like that, all my dread blew away. I rushed inside and found myself in a circular balcony, with only a decorative railing between me and the cathedral floor a world below. There was no one else to be seen, but the song was loud and clear, coming from… There it was! The pocketwatch, lying open on the balcony floor, just a few paces away. The canary's tiny mouth opening and closing and filling the entire dome with its voice.

I hurried forward and stooped to pick it up. My hand never reached it. My eyes were drawn up by the most hideous sight: Wix climbing down a diagonal rope like a monstrous spider in its web.

One end of the rope was tied to a hook in the gallery wall. The other end ran through a pulley at the dome's apex, beneath which hung a large rectangular object. I didn't have to guess what it was.

Wix dropped to the ground, making the balcony quiver beneath my feet. His face was cloaked in shadow, but satisfaction was audible in his rasping voice. "'Ello, girly. Miss me?"

A blade glinted in the dark as Wix bent down, snatched up the pocketwatch, and clamped it shut in his fist, silencing the canary. I walked backwards, feeling frantically for the rail behind me. Wix's grotesque figure came nearer; I could lean back no further without falling. He loomed over me, pressing his monstrous face with its evil sneer and sickening breath so close, it made me lightheaded.

"I'll give ya a choice." He toyed with the end of his knife as he spoke. "You can cooperate nice-like while I ties your 'ands 'n' feet... *or* you can take the long dive down." He leaned further over me to peer over the rail with a wicked chuckle. "Wonder 'ow long it'd take ya to 'it the bottom."

Trembling, I looked around for an escape. Under Wix's armpit, I could see the door, now wide open. *So close.*

As I watched, the tall, lean figure of Phineas Webb stepped through the doorway, then pushed the door closed behind him. I was ambushed.

"Now, now, Mr. Wix. There is no need for such indelicacy. I'm certain our young friend quite understands her situation." He lifted the lantern to his face, and smiled a smile as cold and unfeeling as a stone statue.

29

LEAP OF FAITH

"Gabriel sent you, did he? I believe that's what they call a 'fool's errand'." Phineas stepped closer and held out his hand. Wix placed the pocketwatch in his palm. His fingers curled around it. "I never could understand how my brother inspired such loyalty in people."

I thought I'd better let him believe he was right. If he thought I'd come on Gabriel's orders, he might suspect I had backup, or at least that I knew what I was doing. "He knows the painting on his barge was a fake," I said.

His eyes were fixed on the hanging object above. "Ingenious, is it not?"

"You're not a genius. You're a thief."

His lips curled into that cold smile again as he lowered his eyes to mine. "I, Miss Watson, am a modern-day Leonardo. As you're here, allow me to show you how this little contraption works. Wix–"

Wix exhaled his horrible breath into my face, then straightened up and swaggered over to the hook in the wall. Untying the rope, he gripped it in his gnarly hands and began releasing the slack.

The pulley up above creaked as *The Wedding Feast* descended until it hung just over the railing in front of Phineas, suspended over the distant chequered floor.

He lifted his lantern. It illuminated the rich, deep royal reds and glimmering golds of a royal banquet presided over by a kingly figure. "You see, Miss Watson, had a trained eye inspected the painting discovered on my brother's boat, it would have recognised a slap-dash copy instantly. But I was confident a hard-boiled policeman like Janklow would never recognise the difference."

"He's not a policeman," I said, unable to hide the anger in my voice. "He's a detective, and a brilliant one."

Phineas raised his eyebrows. "So loyal to the man who dismissed you with no more than a simple word from me? Admirable, Miss Watson. But foolish. Loyalty to oneself is the only loyalty that counts in this world."

"Is that what you told Ramona when you locked her up in a tower like one of your caged birds?"

Phineas's smile fell. For the first time, his features showed real emotion. "How could you know..." His eyes narrowed. "Who are you really?"

It was fear written on his features; it made me bold. I knew something he did not. At last I had the upper hand. "I'm not your brother's spy."

The vein beneath Phineas's eye twitched. He waited for me to say more.

Standing tall and squaring him off, I asserted proudly, "I am Ramona's descendant. She has a family. A husband

and a child, and generations of people after her. You can't keep her locked away in your fantasy world."

"How did you come here?"

"The painting you hung up in place of yours. Gabriel didn't paint it. Ramona did. I bet you never guessed it was a time portal."

Phineas's stone façade melted away. A vicious, wild look lit up his eyes; the cold smile became a snarl. "It matters not. Where I am going, there is no husband, no child. They do not exist," he spat. "There, Ramona has only me–"

"She doesn't belong to you!" I shouted in his face, forgetting my fear, I was so angry. "You can't undo the life she's already lived. Can't you see that? I'm proof of it."

Phineas opened his mouth, but quickly closed it again. He studied me like he might study a painting, appraising it for its value. I held my breath, hoping beyond hope my words had struck his heart.

At last, he asked, "Do you have the gift? Do you also paint… the past?"

The way he looked at me, hungrily, made me shudder. "No," I answered.

His face turned frigid again with disappointment. "Then you are of no use to me. And within a few moments, you will be of no threat. When I am gone, you will cease to exist. Ramona will be mine until her dying day. Her descendants will be my descendants. In a matter of time, no one will ever have heard of Katie Watson, nor shall they. But they will hear of Lord Warwick and his Lady Ramona. Our names shall live on through the ages."

The bell struck its first gong. It was midnight.

Phineas took in a sharp breath. "And now I must bid you adieu. My lady awaits me. Wix, see that this child is silenced when I am gone."

With a spasm of twisted laughter, Wix grabbed me by my hair and wrenched me towards the balcony railing.

"Not yet, Wix," Phineas sounded impatient. "Wait until I have gone. Then her death need not weigh upon my conscience."

"What about him?" I screeched as Wix pushed my head over the railing. "He knows your secret, doesn't he? What's to stop *him* telling?"

Phineas laughed. "Even a chimpanzee will obey a command if he's offered a big enough piece of fruit."

Wix stopped trying to lift me by my waist and gave a low growl.

"Besides," Phineas said after another gong of the bell, "who would believe such a great buffoon? My secret is safe with him."

Wix's grip on my hair loosened. I craned my head around to see him scratching his head, trying to decide whether he had just been complimented or insulted.

"Now at last." Phineas's full attention turned to the painting. He spoke to it dreamily, lovingly. "My final farewell to this modern world." His hand went to his pocket; he drew out the canary pocketwatch and held it in his palm.

I took advantage of Wix's momentary distraction to thrust my elbow into his gut. He hurled over and released my hair. I lunged for the pocketwatch, snatching it out of Phineas's opened hand before he knew what had happened.

But before I could turn and bolt for the door, Wix hooked me around the waist and squeezed the air out of my lungs. With his other hand, he grabbed my wrist and crushed it in his fist. I thought it would break, but still I clung on to the watch while tears from the pain blurred my eyes.

"We're wasting time, Wix! I want that watch before the last strike of the clock."

Wix lifted me off the ground and flung me over the railing. I was dangling in midair. One glance over my shoulder and the world started spinning. I could not see or think or breathe. The only thing keeping me from falling was Wix's one hand still gripped around my wrist while his other hand prised the watch from my fingers.

Phineas spoke from above; his voice sounded distant. "At least it will be a quick, painless end. Goodbye, Miss Watson."

The bell tolled again. My freed fingers clung desperately to the railing. I squeezed my eyes shut. Any second, I would hear the canary sing. Phineas would disappear, and I would fall.

But the song did not begin. I heard instead the sound of the door banging open, a shuffling of feet, and someone shouting, "Stand back or I'll shoot!"

My eyes flew open. It was Janklow's voice! I couldn't believe it. He had come to my rescue! But one move from Wix, and I would be beyond rescuing.

Wix, still clasping my wrist, turned his ugly face towards the commotion behind him just in time to meet with a flying fist. My hand slipped from his, but it was caught! I looked up and was looking into Gabriel Webb's face.

"Hang on," Gabriel said, hoisting me up with all his might. Dobbs and Imogen appeared at his side, clinging to any part of me they could reach. In a second, I was over the rail and lying in a heap in Imogen's arms. Gabriel and Dobbs were back on Wix, pinning him face down to the ground.

Imogen braced my arm as I pushed myself up to my feet. My legs wobbled like jelly beneath me, but I wanted to see the look of defeat on Phineas Webb's face.

His expression was stoney again. He looked absolutely calm, even while Janklow's pistol remained trained on him.

"You'll be coming with me, Mr. Webb."

"That's *Sir* Phineas, if you please," he sighed. "Inspector, it is clear that, despite my warning, you have been taken in. Let's be reasonable–"

"No, *Mr.* Webb," Janklow interrupted, and I saw Phineas flinch. "I don't pretend to understand all that is going on here. But I can tell you this. For once, Reason has failed me. Thankfully, the bravery of these young people led me to the light." Without moving his gun, he turned his head and smiled at me. "Good work, Miss Watson. It seems I have a lot to learn from you."

I couldn't yet speak, but I smiled back.

The moment was broken by the sound of shattering glass as Phineas smashed his lantern against the railing. "I am sorry to have to take drastic measures." To my horror, he held the open flame beneath the canvas of *The Wedding*

Feast. It began to smoke; then, all at once, it burst into flame.

"Stop! In the name of the law!" Janklow shouted.

But there was nothing anyone could do. It happened in the blink of an eye. Phineas climbed over the railing and leaned out towards the burning canvas. With one hand he clicked open the pocketwatch. The canary had sung only a few notes when the painting began to move; the king raised a goblet to his lips, unaware that his banquet hall was in flames.

Dobbs shouted, "Law, it's alive!"

Janklow rushed forward.

At the same time, the canary struck a clear, high note. Time seemed to stop for an instant. Then, Phineas stepped out into thin air and...

In a billow of smoke and ash, he was gone.

The painting sagged, as if pulled down by a weight.

"It's going to fall!" I shouted, swinging my leg over the railing. "We've got to go now." Imogen followed my lead. We sat on the rail, holding one another around the waist. "Don't look down," I said.

"Don't do it, Miss Humphreys!" Inspector Janklow called out. "Miss Watson, stay where you are!"

Dobbs was trying to get up, but stumbled over Wix. Gabriel was tying Wix's hands in a flurry.

"We have to!" I called over my shoulder. "Dobbs, Samson is in Bloomsbury Square Gardens. I promised him an apple!"

"Wot? Miss Katie, wot'cha on about? You don't mean to–"

I hated turning my back on them all, but even a moment's hesitation, and it would be too late.

"Are you sure about this, Katie?" Imogen said, her voice high and small.

I couldn't answer, couldn't move. But then the painted queen's eyes met mine. She was wreathed in flame, but she nodded calmly as if to reassure me that all would be okay.

"I'm sure," I answered. "Ready?"

"Yes," she squeaked.

"Wait!" Gabriel was limping towards us, his hand stretched out to pull us back.

"Now!" I shouted.

We leapt, but we never fell. A mighty gust of wind caught us up and spun us in a vortex of flame and flashing colour. Imogen's arm stayed clasped around my waist, and I was just aware of another hand holding fast to my foot. We were not alone.

EPILOGUE

*M*y eyes opened to warm, golden sunlight and tall, sweet-smelling grass. If it was a dream, it was a wonderfully comfortable one.

"AchOO!"

My heart jumped and I sat up. Imogen sat near me in the tall grass; behind her was a perfect Imogen-shaped imprint where she had just been lying.

"At least it's not winter here," she said through watering eyes as she wiped her nose on her sleeve, adding, "Wherever *here* is."

The memory of our death-defying leap from the dome of St. Paul's materialised like a forgotten dream into my mind. It had happened only a moment before, yet it felt long ago and distant. I closed my eyes and tried to picture their faces: Janklow… Dobbs… Gabriel.

"Well, I never thought I'd experience that sensation again," a man's voice said.

Imogen and I both whirled around in disbelief.

Kneeling in the grass, knocking the side of his head with his palm, was Gabriel Webb!

"It was you!" I said, getting up. "You grabbed my foot when we jumped." The idea of Gabriel hanging off my foot in mid-air made me woozy. "That was a mad thing to do," I reprimanded him. "What if you'd fallen?"

He grinned, still rubbing his head. "I might ask the same of you, Miss Watson. Sometimes in life, madness is required of us. But, thank God, here we all are!"

"But you didn't have to come–"

"Oh yes I did." Gabriel heaved himself up and limped forward to offer a hand to Imogen. "I owed it to you, and I owe it to Ramona. It's time I stopped hiding and did what's right. You two girls have shown me that. Besides," – his tone became flat – "I have unfinished business with my brother."

"But what about your barge, and Alph and Billy Bones?" Imogen asked.

Gabriel was squinting into the sun. "I'm not entirely sure they exist at this moment, Miss Humphreys. Though I'm also not entirely sure I understand how this whole time travel business works. But if Alph and Billy Bones need looking after, I feel certain I can rely on Dobbs and Janklow to keep an eye on them."

Dobbs and Janklow. That reminded me of one remaining mystery. "How did you both turn up at St. Paul's, and how on earth did you persuade Janklow to come?"

"Simple, really," Imogen answered. "I told Janklow what had happened. Mrs. Janklow told him if he didn't march straight down to that police station and see that her boy and that 'angelic girl' were brought home safe, she would never cook him another pie in his life."

My mouth hung open. I could barely imagine Mrs. Janklow using such strong language.

"So he came with you? Just like that?"

"I think he would've come, even without Mrs. Janklow's threats. We went straight to Smart, and Janklow insisted on speaking to both Dobbs and Gabriel."

I looked at Gabriel, who picked up the story.

"He was sick with worry about you," he said. "I never would have thought a man like Janklow could let his heart get the better of his resolve, but he was ready to listen to what I had to say if it would help him save you."

"What did you say to him?" I asked, touched that the Inspector cared so much.

"I risked the truth. I told him about the magic paintings... told him what I believed Phineas to be up to. As evidence, I told him the painting on my barge was a fake. He called his man Mortimer for a second opinion. The little man actually laughed when he looked at it. He said a child might have recognised the difference."

"And then Janklow believed you?"

"And then he believed *you*, Miss Watson. He had enough evidence to know that you were, as he always knew deep down, trustworthy."

I bit my lip and looked away, embarrassed to show the tears forcing their way into my eyes.

"Anyway," Imogen continued with a sigh, "Janklow busted Dobbs and Gabriel out, then went straight to look for you at Camelot. When we got there, the manservant said Sir Phineas had gone out, but he wouldn't say where.

Just as we were about to get into the carriage, Willie the Slink turned up on a mule. He said *you* rode up on its back, dismounted in the garden, and hitched the it to a bench before taking off on the back of Phineas's carriage. It was an insane story which, of course, I had no trouble believing. Anyway, Willie rode the mule after you as far as Fleet Street, then turned back."

"That was enough to tell us that Phineas, and you, were headed for St. Paul's," Gabriel explained. "We only hoped we would arrive in time."

"You weren't a minute too soon," I said with a laugh, though my stomach twisted to think just how close they had come to finding me broken on the cathedral floor.

A horn sounded in the distance, turning our heads towards the west, where the sun had dipped beneath the trees. We shaded our eyes against its last rays to look for signs of what, or *who* had made the noise.

"Oh, look!" Imogen pointed to something in the distance. "There's a castle, just rising out of those woods!"

I had just spotted the towers and banners of the castle silhouetted against the western sky when a host of armoured riders spilled out of the woods and down the hillside. Long swords at their sides glinted in the setting sunlight. My heart climbed into my throat as I realised they were riding straight in our direction. They would be on us in minutes, and there was nowhere to hide.

Gabriel stepped in front of us as the leader of the host approached and called for his companions to halt. He held a blue and yellow chequered banner in one fist. With the other hand, he threw up the visor of his helmet.

"Who goes there?" He demanded.

"We are travellers, sir," Gabriel answered. "Where exactly *do* we go, if you please?"

"You have entered the realm of his lordship, the Earl of Warwick, and his lady, soon to be Countess, Ramona."

I looked at Imogen and saw on her face exactly what I felt – relief wrestling with dread. We had done it. We had found Ramona at last! But never before had we been so far from home nor in such a predicament. I felt a rush of gratitude to Gabriel for coming with us.

"If you seek lodgings for the night in the castle keep, might I urge you to hasten forthwith," the horseman said a little impatiently. "The portcullis gate will close at sunset."

Gabriel bowed. "Thank you, sir."

"Ride on!" the man ordered his party.

Instantly, the ground quivered as the horses bucked up and sped away, leaving no more than a cloud of dust behind. As the riders became smaller in the distance and the sound of hooves died away, Imogen and I turned to each other, both letting out a breath of relief in unison.

"Welcome to the age of chivalry," she said, making jazz hands.

I shook my head, but I was glad she had hung on to her sense of humour after all we'd been through. She would never know just how much I needed it.

"Not long before sunset." Gabriel shielded his eyes and squinted towards the castle.

"I'm ready if you are," I said. Gabriel nodded. Imogen linked her arm through mine, and together we started off towards the setting sun. Towards Ramona.

Whatever dangers awaited, I could be confident of one thing: when I met them, I would not be alone.

Join the Katie Watson Fan Club!

Sign up for Mez Blume's Newsletter
and be the first to hear about
Katie Watson Official News,
Bonus Features, Announcements,
Contests, Givaways & more.

Visit
MezBlume.com
to join &
download
a FREE
audiobook!

VICTORIAN GLOSSARY

Truncheon – a wooden club carried by policemen

'Bricky' – slang word meaning plucky, brave or fearless

Workhouse – a poorhouse in which paupers and orphans were given work for lodgings

Hostel for Girls of Good Character – a charitable lodging for poor or destitute young women

Omnibus – the Victorian version of a public, horse-drawn 'bus'

Arcade – an arched, covered passageway with shops on either side (e.g. Covent Garden Market)

Skilamalimk – someone who is secretive, shady or sneaky

Hansom Cab – a small horse-drawn, two-wheeled carriage popular for transport in London

Penny Dreadful – one-penny magazines published weekly; featured sensational, often frightful adventures

Ha'penny – pronounced '*hay*-penny'; an abbreviation of 'half penny'

Shilling – a silver coin worth 12 pence in British currency

Crown – a silver coin worth 5 shillings

Constable – starting rank for an officer of the London Metropolitan Police Force, est. 1829

Bobbies/Coppers – slang words for policemen

'Got the morbs' – slang to describe someone who is gloomy or melancholy

'Slip through his daddles' – criminal slang meaning to escape capture, or 'slip through his fingers'

'Back slang it' – criminal slang for 'go out the back way'

'Spreadin' butter on bacon' – slang for 'overdoing it'

Monocle – a single eye glass used to closely examine something

Mop-cap – a gathered, cloth bonnet worn by women at home and house maids

River Barge/ Canal Boat – a long, narrow, flat-bottomed boat designed to navigate canals. Also referred to as a 'narrowboat'

ACKNOWLEDGMENTS

No book belongs to the author alone. This one was born from the help and inspiration of a whole host of wonderful people.

Thank you, Bri Stox, for having the courage and kindness to wade through the first messy draft and actually like it! Without that confidence boost, this book would probably still be languishing on the shelf. Many thanks to my invaluable editor, Anna Bowles. Truly, neither I nor Katie Watson could get off the ground without you. Accolades are due to my two proofreaders: Ruth Smith, who brandished her grammatical double-edged sword to vanquish many an error, and my mom, Mary Blume, who would not rest until every misspelled word had been put to rights. My hat is off to creative mastermind Patrick Knowles once again for another glowing cover.

A hearty round of applause for my Advance Readers and Loyal Katie Fans:

Asher Parham; Jim Blume; Gordon Stead; Marion, Tamsyn & Ethan Alston; Sheryl Bake; Deb, Josiah, Ember, Sage & Grace Richards; Susan & Aurelia Beattie; Mark Smith; Michelle Fidler; Fiona & Izzy Kennedy; Rachael, Amelia, Anna & Andrew Grant; Alex Thaxton; Linda Gore; Katherine George; Jenifer Dunn; Ruth Nelson; Alice & Florence Bolton; Kane Kanavage; Danny Delgado; Jo Wallis; Zizzie Knowles; Kelly Brockett; & Michael Dormandy.

Thanks to my husband, Gordon. Dobbs has you to thank for his heart of gold and love for dogs.

And finally, thanks to Ye Olde City of London – my home for eight years – for providing me with so much fodder for this book and many other books besides. And special thanks to St Paul's Cathedral, where some rather important bits of this story take place. Visit there if you can, but be advised! View mysterious, moving paintings at your own risk…

ABOUT THE AUTHOR

Mez Blume is the British-American author of the celebrated first three books in the *Katie Watson Mysteries in Time* series. With two more 'Katie books' due to release, she has, like Katie, become a frequent 'time traveller', often venturing into history in search of ideas for her next story. You can sign up for Mez's official Newsletter at MezBlume.com.

- facebook.com/mezblume
- twitter.com/mez_blume
- instagram.com/mez_blume

www.ingramcontent.com/pod-product-compliance
Lightning Source LLC
Chambersburg PA
CBHW020521080526
44583CB00013B/691